PLANTS & GARDENS

BROOKLYN BOTANIC GARDEN RECORD

Ornamental Grasses

1988

Brooklyn Botanic Garden

Staff for this issue:

PETER LOEWER, *Guest Editor*

BARBARA B. PESCH, *Editor*

CHARLES GABELER, *Art Director*

JO KEIM, *Associate Editor*

and the Editorial Committee of the Brooklyn Botanic Garden

DONALD E. MOORE, *President, Brooklyn Botanic Garden*

ELIZABETH SCHOLTZ, *Director Emeritus*

STEPHEN K-M. TIM, *Vice President, Science & Publications*

First printing, September 1988

Second printing, revised, September 1989

PLANTS & GARDENS
BROOKLYN BOTANIC GARDEN RECORD

Ornamental Grasses

Vol. 44   Fall 1988   Handbook #117   No. 3

CONTENTS

Pennisetum setaceum *combined with begonias at Longwood Gardens.*
Cover photograph and all others unless otherwise indicated by Elvin McDonald

Plants and Gardens, Brooklyn Botanic Garden Record (ISSN 0362-5850) is published quarterly at 1000 Washington Ave., Brooklyn, N.Y. 11225, by the **Brooklyn Botanic Garden, Inc.** Second-class-postage paid at Brooklyn, N.Y., and at additional mailing offices. Subscriptions included in Botanic Garden membership dues ($20.00 per year), which includes newsletters and announcements. Copyright •1989 by the Brooklyn Botanic Garden, Inc.
POSTMASTER: Send address changes to BROOKLYN BOTANIC GARDEN, Brooklyn, N.Y. 11225

foreword

Peter Loewer

The grasses, *Gramineae* to the botanist, represent the most important single plant family on earth, since they alone produce all the cereal grains that have sustained humanity throughout recorded history. This handbook deals with a very small segment of the over 10,000 cataloged species: those grown for ornament in home and garden. Popular in Europe and Asia for years, the ornamental grasses have been largely overlooked by the American gardener in favor of plants that are thought to be showier in form and color. If the American public knows the ornamental grasses at all, it's as dried accompaniment to winter bouquets.

In Japan and China, where gardens have been appreciated for thousands of years, it is no longer important how many plant varieties one can grow, but rather how many facets one can see in a single plant. Theirs is a culture that finds restful contemplation in gardens made entirely of mosses, grasses or stones. And grasses truly lend themselves to such an examination.

Today, our culture is a mobile one, and because of economic demands the typical family no longer settles in one place for its entire existence, and few people bother with the less flamboyant or slower growing members of the plant world. Instead, we demand the fast and the blatant bloom, and thus the graceful grasses are relegated to the lawn for cutting and the gift shops of colonial Williamsburg, where as dried flowers, they remind us of our agricultural past.

At this point I'm reminded of two memories: The first was my initial glimpse of a mature clump of zebra grass in Paula Roos's twenty-year-old garden in Honesdale, Pennsylvania, and the majesty it commanded; the second is the following story of two American visitors touring an English estate:

"Goodness, me," said one as they trod the palatial lawn, "this grass is magnificent," and turning to the head gardener, asked: "How do you get a beautiful lawn like this?"

"Well, ma'am," he said, "first you roll it for three hundred years." ⟶

Miscanthus sinensis 'Zebrinus' is striped horizontally which creates an unusual effect. It prefers wet soil, stands shoulder high and is topped in autumn and winter with feathery plumes.

A Garden of Grasses

Here in the country's heart
Where the grass is green,
Life is the same sweet life
As it e'er hath been.

Norman Gale,
The Country Faith

*The present is mere grass,
quick-mown away—*

Eugene Lee-Hamilton

Spartina pectinata, *cord grass, is a common
grass that adds a graceful note to the landscape.
It prefers a damp spot and has a variegated form.*

Drawing by Peter Loewer

Peter Loewer

I've been growing ornamental grasses in the garden for over eight years. By the end of August, eulalia grass is often over 10 feet tall, reed grass reaching to 15, Japanese blood grass is turning deep red, goldentop shimmers with silken gilt, blue fescue forms eight-inch clumps of steely blue, and spike rush is one inch tall. They are all beautiful.

Unfortunately at the same time that the garden is a graceful jumble of abstract lines, the lawn is a scraggly two inches higher than it should be and badly needs a trim.

It's difficult to realize that they all belong to the same family, the *Gramineae,* a family that probably represents the single most important group of plants in the world.

For rice, wheat, oats, corn, bamboo, barley, rye, sorghum and sugar are all related. In their seeds and foliage are stored the starches, sugars and vitamins needed to keep humanity alive and healthy.

And it's also the family that contains crabgrass and 274 other common names for 274 individual species that have been in commerce —or backyards—at one time or another.

Annual ornamental grasses are usually grown for their seed panicles—flowers are minute and hardly noticeable—many of which dry beautifully for winter bouquets. Their leaves are usually not too showy.

Perennial grasses have magnificent and varied foliage in all shades of green, blue, and variegations of cream, white, gold, or a host of tans, in addition to notable seed heads.

Sizes run the gamut from tiny to huge, they belong in every garden and if you have the room, they make an impressive garden all their own.

Included in this garden are a few plants that are usually thought of as grasses but really belong to closely allied but more primitive families: the sedges and the rushes.

A Garden of Perennial Grasses

This garden of grasses is planned for a plot measuring 10 by 20 feet. It features 15 species or cultivars of the perennial grasses (including two tropical varieties), one bamboo, and one sedge, for a total of 17 different plants. You might think this is a small number of plants for such a large piece of ground? It isn't! The grasses take a lot of room.

If you want to get some of the feeling of walking through a jungle, plant a thicket of eulalia grass or ravenna grass. By summer's end you will be amazed at the size of these grasses. Three years of active growth are needed before these plants approach their ultimate size.

Ornamental grasses grow in average garden soil. Remove the turf, then turn the earth to a depth of one foot. Add a mix of clean garden soil and some composted manure to make up for the lost earth. Plants do best (except for sea oats) in full sun.

The only real chore in dealing with grasses is the annual pruning of the larger types in early spring. Cut the dead stems and leaves to within six inches of the ground before new growth begins.

The larger clump-forming grasses grow from the inside out so plants die out in the center after a few years. Then divide the clumps with an ax, and pass on extra plants to other gardeners. These plants are not fragile.

Peter Loewer, guest editor of this handbook, is a botanical artist and scientific illustrator who writes magazine articles, and writes and illustrates his own books on gardening. His most recent is The Annual Garden *and he is now at work on a book entitled* American Gardens.

Plants for the Grass Garden

In the following descriptions, the height given is that of the plant in bloom, when the plumes usually stand above the leaves. Except for the tropicals, they are all hardy in Zone 5. Those that can live in Zone 4 are so marked. The first measurement is the height and the second the spread of the plant, in inches.

At Wave Hill, a beautiful formal garden in the Bronx, New York, there is a specimen of ravenna grass planted in solid rock. Blasting two and one-half feet of rock was required to make the hole. The effort was worthwhile: the grass, both in leaf and in bloom, is spectacular! That grass is the center of the planting with others grouped—according to height—around it. The plan also includes a short path of stone that would be an ideal place for a sundial or a spot to summer out the tropical grasses.

The first grass is a bamboo *(Arundinaria viridistriata),* that is hardy with protection in Zone 5, where it is not invasive. Farther south care must be taken in planting to prevent unwanted spread. This bamboo is a true beauty: the leaves have a velvety look when new and are a rich combination of gold and green that glows in the distance. The stems reach a height of two and one-half feet. It prefers partial shade and I find it does best when grown in a 12-inch pot.

Japanese sedge grass *(Carex morrowii* var. *expallida),* 18 by 8 inches, is hardy in Zone 5 but cover with evergreen branches or other loose mulch for the winter. Provide shade from the noonday sun in summer. The gracefully arched leaves are striped with creamy white and green. Flowers resemble camel's-hair brushes dipped in yellow powder and appear in spring.

Northern sea oats *(Chasmanthium latifolium),* 36 by 24 inches, will also tolerate some shade. It is still listed as *Uniola latifolia* in many catalogs. This is a beautiful plant with flat panicles of drooping flowers that are green at first but turn a golden brown after a severe frost. If started from seed, sea oats will not grow with gusto until the second year.

Lemon grass *(Cymbopogon citratus),* 36 by 12 inches, is only hardy in Zone 10, but can be grown in a pot in northern climates. It will rarely exceed three feet when grown indoors but can top six feet in the tropics. The flower, if it blooms, is nondescript, but the plant is very attractive with its arching leaves of light green. Lemon grass is the commercial source of lemon oil, and a crushed leaf sends forth a wonderful aroma. Plant in light soil with plenty of sand for good drainage. Take indoors for winter in cold areas.

Ravenna grass *(Erianthus ravennae),* 10 to 11 by 5 feet, is the tallest of grasses so some thought should go into its placement. The leaves form a fountain of green that change to a rich brown in early autumn. Then silvery-beige plumes appear. Add composted manure to the soil before planting.

Blue fescue *(Festuca ovina* var. *glauca),* 18 by 10 inches, is hardy in Zone 4. It is a variety of sheeps' fescue grass and has a bluish bloom, which is actually a powder that covers the leaf-blade surfaces and will easily rub off. The name is derived from the Celtic word *fest,* meaning pasture. Plant these grasses in clusters and use them to fill up any vacant spots. The clumps are easily divided when they become too large. Flowers are rather small; the color and shape of the leaves is the chief reason for cultivation.

Japanese blood grass *(Imperata cylindrica rubra),* 18 by 12 inches, is hardy to Zone 5 with winter protection from freezing winds. I solved the problem of exposure by placing the plants in front of a low wall. In the plan an uneven space with a three-foot diameter is set aside for this grass. The reason for cultivating this grass is the color: rich, blood-red that starts about midway on the grass blade and reaches to the tip. Japanese blood grass is fairly new to this country. It has never flowered for me: I think the season just isn't long enough.

Chinese silver grass *(Miscanthus floridulis),* 8 by 3 feet, sits next to eulalia grass in the plan

Erianthus ravennae, ravenna grass, is the tallest of grasses (10 to 11 feet tall by 5 feet wide) so must be placed with care. The leaves form a fountain of green in spring and summer changing to rich brown in autumn when silvery-beige plumes appear.

8

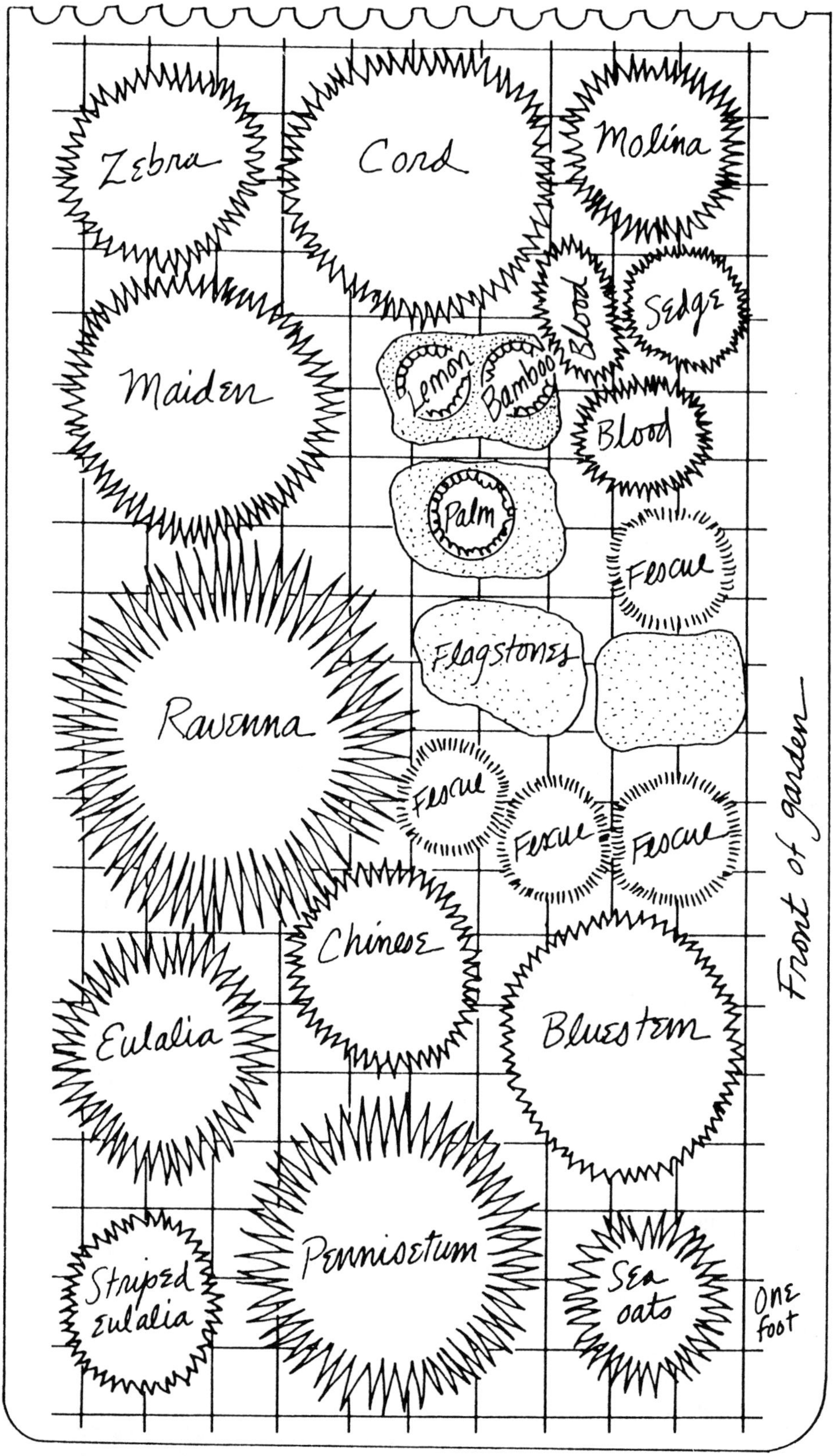

Zebra

Cord

Molina

Maiden

Lemon

Bamboo

Blood

Sedge

Blood

Palm

Fescue

Ravenna

Flagstones

Fescue

Fescue

Fescue

Chinese

Bluestem

Eulalia

Striped eulalia

Pennisetum

Sea oats

Front of garden

One foot

as it's the shorter of the two. They are alike, except for stature.

Eulalia grass (M. *sinensis*), 10 by 3 feet, is a genus of ornamental grasses extensively cultivated throughout the world. These grasses grow very tall and produce magnificent plumes of silvery spikelets with a purple sheen and are much like the feathers carried by Egyptian slaves to fan Cleopatra. As the summer progresses, the bottom leaves die back, and by tearing them off the handsome stems are revealed. These stems become very dark and hard with age and exposure to weather. After the growing season is over, the stems can be cut and polished. In ancient Japan they were used to make many implements: brush handles, kitchen utensils, and tools for print making. If your growing season is less than 90 days, eulalia grass may not flower, but it's worth growing for the leaves alone.

Maiden grass (M. *sinensis* 'Gracillimus'), six by four feet, is aptly named—both its common and cultivar names—since the plant reflects the charm of a graceful maiden. Leaves are light green, with a white mid-rib, long, narrow and lightly curved at the tips.

Zebra grass (M. *sinensis* 'Zebrinus'), six by three feet, is another favorite of mine: individual leaves are dashed with horizontal bands of a light golden brown. A clump can become massive over many years and resembles a sparkling fountain. Zebra grass, like others of the *Miscanthus* tribe, prefers damp soil so it's excellent for the poolside.

Striped eulalia grass (M. *sinensis* 'Variegatus'), five by three feet, is the variegated form and its leaves are heavily striped with white.

Fountain grass *(Pennisetum alopecuroides)*, three by four and one-half feet, has a very wide

A plan for a garden of grasses using those described in this article. This garden resembles that of the guest editor—photographs of which appear in other places in this handbook.

Miscanthus sinensis 'Zebrinus', zebra grass, has individual leaves dashed with horizontal bands of light golden brown. A clump can become massive, resembling a sparkling fountain.

spread—its leaves and flowering stems arch toward the ground. The blossoms are especially beautiful when covered with dew and lit by the morning sun. Fountain grass is effective when placed next to a planting of little bluestem, for the reddish stems of the second plant echo the russet tones of the first. Leave enough room for the plant's spread.

Little bluestem *(Schizachyrium scoparium),* four by four feet, is still listed in many catalogs as *Andropogon scoparius.* It's the state grass of Nebraska. The flowering stems turn a golden reddish-brown in the fall sparked with tiny white tufted blossoms along their edge.

Palm grass *(Setaria palmifolia)* is a slender tropical grass that reaches six feet in a warm climate. The plaited leaves are two feet long and three inches wide, and a deep emerald green. The plants grow well in containers but require full sun outdoors in summer to thrive. I grow palm grass in a 14-inch pot.

Cord grass *(Spartina pectinata* var. *aurea variegata),* five by four feet, has many common names: bull grass, tall marsh grass, slough grass (*slough* is an old Anglo-Saxon word meaning a wet or marshy place), freshwater cord grass, and upland creek grass. American pioneers used this grass to thatch roofs and protect haystacks against the weather. This variegated form of the common grass is quite graceful in the landscape, with bending leaves striped with light tan. As its many names suggest, cord grass does well in a damp spot.

Purple moor grass

The *Dictionary of Gardening* compiled by the Royal Horticultural Society (of England) has the following entry for purple moor grass:

Molina (in honor of Juan Ignacio Molina, 1740-1829, writer on the natural history of Chile). Fam. *Gramineae.* A genus of perhaps two species, one spread over Europe, Asia Minor, and N. Asia, the other Japanese. Perennial

Miscanthus sinensis 'Gracillimus' is a lovely grass with graceful light green leaves with a white mid-rib—long, narrow and lightly colored at the tips.

densely tufted grass with slender leaves. . . A grass of bleak, wet moorlands, the variegated form of which is a good bedding plant; propagated by division.

"Bleak, wet moorlands," and "a good bedding plant," what telling phrases and so English, such understatement for a grass that should be in every garden.

And especially interesting since its one of the few grasses where actual outdoor observations have documented early stages of germination.

In 1915, T.A. Jefferies, wrote the following: *On the moors about Huddersfield . . . little peat hollows, sometimes only about two square feet in area, are common; these become pools in wet weather, but are robbed of their surface water by a few days' drought. Bright sunshine and strong wind playing on the unprotected surface of such a hollow, cause the formation of a network of cracks. Into these the seeds of* Molina *are blown, and are sheltered there from the wind. When the water has disappeared in the early summer, lines of crowded seedlings appear, marking out the meshwork of last season's cracks like miniature green hedgerows.*

Later, Jefferies points out that the root system of *Molina* is particularly notable for the firmness of its roots, making it difficult to pull up from the ground. It is also noted that the swollen nodes at the base of the plant were often used as pipecleaners and toothpicks while the dried stems went into local broom manufacture.

While I cannot testify to the germination I can note its tenacious hold upon the soil, and also to its beauty of the variegated form.

We have had it in the garden since 1978. Each year the fountain of rather rigid leaves, each banded with white stripes and gently curving towards the ground, becomes a little larger and more impressive. The panicles occur atop curving stems and reach three feet in height and are striped like the leaves but tinged with violet and greenish highlights.

Unlike most grasses, *Molina* will tolerate some shade, prefers an acid soil and will put up with some dampness. And that fibrous and tough root system, makes it an excellent plant for banks, and steep hillsides.

If forced to choose, choose this plant.

Establishing a Prairie Grass Garden

Margaret Stock

The American prairies were originally flat, grass-covered and treeless plains that stretched from western Ohio, through Indiana, Illinois, and Iowa, to the Great Plains. Because of the richness of the soil they are not prime producers of crops.

—P.L.

When you plant a mini-prairie in your backyard, you will be planting a bit of history. The early pioneers migrated across the plains in their prairie schooners—wagons covered by a canopy of white canvas—and found the vast grasslands, abundant with wildflowers, ready to be broken by the farmer's plow. The farmers discovered rich, fertile soil, that today produces the food that feeds America.

We can't bring back the prairie as it was centuries ago, but you can plant an area in your own backyard that will resemble one. Enjoy the wildflowers—blanketflower, cornflower, black-eyed Susan, upright coneflower, purple prairie clover, partridge pea, dame's rocket, thickspike, gayfeather and purple coneflower—as they bloom from spring into fall. And of course the grasses. Some of the flowers are annuals and will bloom the first year while others are perennial and may not bloom until the second spring or summer. The grasses for a prairie garden are all perennials.

The grasses take a bit of patience. Little bluestem *(Schizachyrium scoparium)*, side-oats grama *(Bouteloua curtipendula)*, Indian grass *(Sorghastum nutans)*, and blue grama *(Bouteloua gracilis)*, are all busy putting down roots for the first year, roots that grow so

Margaret Stock is a member of the Stock family, owners and operators of Stock Seed Farms, Inc., in Mursock, Nebraska. They maintain 700 acres of grasses and 25 acres of wildflowers for seed production and grow 36 varieties of grasses and wildflowers.

14

deeply that the plants were able to withstand the prairie fires that would rage across the landscape.

Plant the seed in the spring through the early summer. Or plant late enough in the fall so that the seeds will not germinate until the following spring. Remember that prairie plants are not adapted to shade so pick a site that receives full to partial sun and is well drained.

Prepare a seedbed that is free of grass and weeds. The clean seedbed should be firm, not fluffy. Broadcast seed evenly and rake in lightly to a maximum depth of one-eighth inch. Don't worry if some seed shows on the surface of the soil.

The seeds need plenty of water to germinate. Keep the seedbed moist for four to six weeks. Reduce the frequency of watering as the plants become established. After they are entrenched, little care will be needed. Be sure to water when drought conditions exist.

Big bluestem *(Andropogon gerardii)* grows between four and five feet tall and is often called the "king" of native grasses. After frost, this sod-forming grass turns a light reddish-purple.

Blue grama *(Bouteloua gracilis)* grows three to six inches high. It is a long-lived grass that has white-purplish spikelets or flags on each stem.

Indian grass *(Sorghastrum nutans)* is five to eight feet tall, and waves its golden, plumelike head in September making it one of the most beautiful of native grasses.

Reed canary grass *(Phalaris arundinacea)* grows two to four feet tall and is especially suited for wetlands and waterside plantings.

Sand love grass *(Eragrostis trichodes)* only reaches about one foot in height but has lovely purplish, feathery seed heads, growing best on sandy soil.

Switchgrass *(Panicum virgatum)* grows four to five feet high, has beautiful seed heads, and turns a lovely orange-yellow color in winter.

Native Ornamental Grasses

Agnes Chase

Mrs. Mary Agnes Chase was an Honorary Fellow of the Smithsonian Institution and a dean of American agrostologists. She was the author of *First Book of Grasses* published by the Smithsonian and an accomplished botanical illustrator. The following article was taken from *The National Horticultural Magazine* for January, 1928.

When one speaks of ornamental grasses a mental picture arises of a great clump of eulalia *(Miscanthus sinensis)* like a spouting volcano in the middle of a lawn, or of rather unsightly tussocks of ribbon grass *(Phalaris arundinacea picta)*, or at best of fountain grass *(P. setaceum)* with its faintly rosy panicles, surrounding circular beds of cannas in city parks. Giant reed grass *(Arundo donax)* and pampas grass *(C. selloana)* are also commonly grown in great clumps in our parks. None of these, except *P. setaceum,* approaches in grace and beauty a large number of our native grasses.

For a bold clump in the open, our perennial Indian grass *(S. avenaceum)* with its stately stems four to five feet high would be far more handsome than eulalia. It is not so coarse; the clumps are not a dense mass but more open and graceful. The long tapering upright golden-bronze panicles appear in early September and last about a month, turning russet toward maturity. This grass is widespread, from the northern Atlantic states to the foothills of the Rockies. In a garden or park it would be effective toward the back of a perennial border or at the margin of shrubbery, at a corner or sharp curve. This grass does not make rapid growth early in the season, being only about three feet high in early August,

Agnes Chase became interested in botany at an early age and while in Chicago, worked at night as a proofreader on the Inter-Ocean *newspaper and botanized during the day. In 1936, she became the senior botanist in charge of all systematic agrostology at the United States Department of Agriculture.*

Sorghastrum nutans, *Indian grass, has
stately stems sometimes reaching five feet in
height. The clumps are open and graceful. The
golden panicles appear in early September.*

Drawing by Peter Loewer

hence is better adapted to borders or corners than to use in open lawns.

Another native species for borders in such places as ribbon grass is used is wild rye *(Elymus canadensis)*. This is also widespread and hardy from the Atlantic nearly to the Rockies. The stems stand about three feet high and from July to September bear nodding heads five or six inches long, with long slender curving bristles. The leaves are about half-an-inch long and graceful.

Hystrix patula, *bottlebrush grass, has gray stems, spreading leaves and long-awned spike-lets. The drawing on the opposite page illustrates the size of this grass.*

Purpletop *(Triodia flava)* with very smooth foliage and handsome large drooping purple panicles, blooming during August and September, is found from southern New England to Missouri and southward. It can be used in a sterile bit of soil where other plants do not thrive. It is particularly charming back of Michaelmas daisies and our other native asters.

The most beautiful of our native grasses is broadleaf uniola *(Chasmanthium latifolium)*. It grows in low woods from Pennsylvania to eastern Kansas and southward, but is not nearly so common as the species mentioned above. Though a woodland grass it flourishes in open sunlight. Some ten years ago I brought a clump from near the Potomac and set it in my garden. It has thrived without any care at all and has furnished clumps for neighbors and friends. Its graceful stems, three to four feet high, broad spreading leaves, and drooping panicles of large very flat spikelets, are charming in a perennial border or at the margin of shrubbery. The plant is also effective in shaded ground under trees and tall shrubs. The panicles appear in early August and last fully two months. A single stem with its graceful panicle or a few in a slender vase, or a greater number arranged in a standard in a broad flat bowl, are very decorative in the house. (Editor's note: these are the only ornamental grasses whose seed heads retain their green color when dried.)

For those fortunate enough to have wooded slopes or a bit of rich woods there are several elegant native grasses besides uniola. In the northern states *Milium effusum,* with tall slender pale stems, broad leaves, and graceful delicate panicles of small whitish spikelets, would add beauty to shaded ground.

Our native woodland brome grasses *(B. canadensis* and close relatives) are found throughout the northern states and southward. They grow in small tufts, the slender stems four to six feet tall, with graceful foliage and drooping panicles of long spikelets.

Woodreed *(Cinna arundinacea)* is found in moist spots in about the same area. It is less slender than the bromes and has a large nodding, rather dense grayish-green panicle of small spikelets. It would make itself at home along a

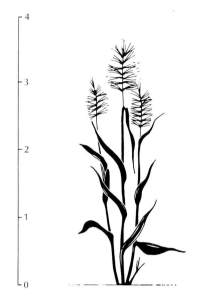

rivulet or drain or where *Iris pseudacorus* thrives. *Elymus striatus,* one of the wild-rye grasses, growing on banks above streams with drooping pale heads of spikelets with delicate curving bristles, would thrive in the same situations.

Bottlebrush grass *(Hystrix patula)* is already cultivated to some extent, but deserves wider use. On an open wooded slope a colony of *Hystrix* with its slender gray stems, spreading leaves, and swaying heads of horizontally spreading long-awned spikelets, suggests a dance of the nymphs.

Any of the broad-leaved panic grasses *(Panicum clandestinum, P. latifolium, P. boscii)* produce good foliage effects in perennial borders. In spring and early summer these have simple stems two to three feet tall and small panicles of little round spikelets. In midsummer the stems begin to branch, the upper joints fall away, the branches multiply and by September the effect is that of a miniature shrubby bamboo, quite Japanese in feel. They are picturesque beside a flight or two or three steps or at the end of a path. These grasses have the peculiar habit of producing close-fertilized seeds which remain enclosed in the sheaths. The chickadees feast on the seeds in winter.

The New Ornamental Grasses

Cortaderia selloana, *pampas grass, is a striking grass that is best used alone. It cannot be successfully grown where the temperature regularly falls below 10°F. The grass is drawn to scale on page 23.*

Drawings by Peter Loewer

One of the first nurserymen and gardeners in the U.S. to popularize the ornamental grasses and bamboos, describes some of the new cultivars coming on the market.　　—P.L.

Kurt Bluemel

In the last five years I have devoted a great deal of effort to introducing new ornamental grasses to the already growing number of varieties.

My effort has been directed at collecting and selecting good cultivars of *Miscanthus*. I also find it very important to make these new selections available to the public and the trade. *Miscanthus,* the ones we know, bloom late in the season (October-November). The flowers do not reach over the foliage and the colors of inflorescence are not very showy. At this time I am comparing over fifty species, varieties and selections of the genus *Miscanthus*.

Miscanthus 'Graziella' is a vastly improved selection of *M. sinensis* with narrow leaves, long stems and large silvery inflorescence well above the foliage, forming white seed heads reminiscent of ostrich plumes.

M. 'Malepartus' is very similar in habit but has a wider leaf. Both varieties bloom as early as the middle of August and reach six to seven feet when mature. It is winter hardy to USDA Zone 5. Both varieties have very good fall color.

M. 'Arabesque' is a dwarf selection three and one-half to four feet, early blooming (August) with golden inflorescence.

Kurt Bluemel owns a nursery in Maryland and supplies most of the ornamental grass plants used in the nursery and landscaping business today. He continually searches for the new and the unusual in grasses and other perennial plants.

M. 'Sarabande' is a selection of *M.* 'Gracillimus' with a strong silver stripe in the middle of the leaf. This plant has a slender elegant appearance, blooming in September with silvery inflorescences and a mature height of five and one-half to six feet.

All the above selections are a great improvement over the *Miscanthus* offered in the trade so far; they are a different generation of the Japanese silver grass.

The following *Miscanthus* are of a different nature. The National Arboretum in Washington, D.C. made two very interesting variegated *Miscanthus* available for propagation.

M. 'Cabaret' is a broadleaf variegated selection, the white stripes running lengthwise on the leaf. Almost 70 percent of the leaf surface is white. Because it is so light, this plant can be successfully used against a dark background. It lightens a dark area, not unlike a garden light. The maximum height is four to five feet and the flowers are late (October). The plant is not used for the flowers but the foliage. It is hardy to Zone 6.

My favorite *Miscanthus* is the variety 'Morning Light'. I remember from old publications the name *"Miscanthus sinensis gracillimus variegatus",* which is very musical but unwieldy. The name 'Morning Light' describes the silvery glistening foliage, the narrow sharp leaves arching gracefully. The plant attains four to five feet in height and blooms in late fall (October). This *Miscanthus* is also planted for its foliage and would be beautiful in a "gray" garden; work it well with the blues, like *Veronica incana* or *Caryopteris* or *Perovskia*. Hardy in Zone 5, 'Morning Light' will make many friends in the future.

The following two varieties of *Miscanthus* are for the plant lover with a small garden area. *M.* 'Yaku Jima' from the island of Japan with the same name, grows three- to four-feet tall at maturity, blooming in the beginning of August with foliage that is narrow and silvery and has golden flowers. Safe to plant in Zone 7. Two clones are offered in the trade, one is more compact than the above mentioned. A very attractive use for this small *Miscanthus* is in between *Aster dumosus*, heather or heath, or other low-growing perennials.

M. transmorrisonensis, named after Mt. Morrison in Taiwan, is very graceful and reaches three to four feet maximum height and blooms in July with golden inflorescences that will sway in the gentlest breeze. The plant can be successfully used as a hedge or specimen plant in a perennial border, or used in large drifts to create a dramatic landscape picture in combination with masses of *Sedum* 'Autumn Joy' or *Sedum* 'Ruby Glow'; *Coreopsis* 'Zagreb' or *Coreopsis* 'Moonbeam'; *Rudbeckia* 'Goldsturm'; *Perovskia*; or lower-growing ornamental grasses such as *Helictotrichon, Sesleria, Festuca* or *Pennisetum* 'Hameln'. It is hardy in Zone 7.

Other new introductions are:

Imperata 'Red Baron' *(Imperata cylindrica rubra)* is making its successful entrance into many gardens. This 12- to 18-inch-high plant with brilliant red foliage looks best when backlit by the evening sun. Large plantings in combination with a chartreuse color grass *(Sesleria autumnalis)* or a yellow variety, *Hakonechloa macra aureola, Carex* 'Evergold', or *Alopecurus pratensis aureus* give a remarkable effect. *Imperata* does well in full sun and part shade. The grasslike

Ophiopogon planiscapus 'Arabicus' is also a good plant to use in concert with 'Red Baron'; both are hardy in Zone 6.

Pampas grass, *Cortaderia,* from Argentina is not dependably winter hardy in Zone 7. *Cortaderia pumila* has been the hardiest pampas grass in Zone 7. It has survived many winters here in Maryland. This plant is valuable because it is only five to six feet tall and is a strong blooming selection, even a one year division will produce five to eight inflorescences the first year. It is a good specimen plant and can be used for cut flowers. This *Cortaderia* will be used frequently in the future.

Bamboos are all true grasses. Popular belief is that bamboos are the most invasive plants on this earth and this is partially true. There are hardy varieties that are not invasive called *Sinarundinaria*. These beautiful bamboos attain a height of 10 to 15 feet, are clump forming and hardy to minus 20° F. They tolerate a good deal of shade.

Bamboos, as a whole, are very graceful plants with their foliage and culms. An effort should be made to use this diverse plant to advantage. Invasive bamboos can be controlled by a running brook, concrete sidewalks, buildings or good structural elements buried to a depth of 30 inches. Deep shade will also hamper the rapid spread of some bamboos.

An established stand of bamboos creates a microclimate. Many animals and birds will make it their home.

Bamboo ground covers (Arundinarias and Sasas) are equally usable. Between walks, median strips, buildings and in hard-to-maintain areas, ground bamboos are hardy plants. The only maintenance required is cutting them back once a year and removing all the debris. Use the invasiveness to your advantage! Some bamboos make good house plants, such as *Phyllostachys nigra*.

The names of bamboos are also causing a great deal of confusion. *Sinarundinaria* has had three name changes in as many years

(*Thamnocalamus, Fargesia*). Both of the following varieties are useful as specimen plants.

Sinarundinaria murielea is well suited for a shady spot. The true bright green color of the foliage is graceful and shows very well in the shade. The green slender stem, approximately three-fourths inch in diameter, arches gracefully. Few evergreen 'grasses' grow well in shade.

S. nitida is different because of its bluish appearance. The stems can vary in color but the purplish hue is prevalent. Stem diameter is three-fourths to one inch. This variety has a more upright growth habit. In winter when temperatures dip below freezing, their leaves will roll up like the leaves of the rhododendron.

Patience is needed when planting *Sinarundinaria*. It will take five to seven years to obtain a specimen plant of 10 to 15 feet in height. It is worth waiting for because few plants will rival their grace.

Cortaderia selloana

Gardening with Bamboo

by Elvin McDonald

Bamboo, whether dead or alive, remains one of the most-wanted plants in the world. It is inextricably linked with things oriental, yet a staple in the most Western of gardens. Hardly any serious gardener does without bamboo stakes and living bamboos come in all sizes and for all climates, from tropical to temperate where, with protection, the hardiest survive cold ranging from minus 10 to minus 20 degrees F. Richard Haubrich of the American Bamboo Society* recommends that bamboo be used as a hedge, a screen, as a specimen or as a shade plant. The introduction to bamboo that follows is based on information from Thomas Brothers Nursery (Cameron, N.C. 28326, a chief supplier of bamboo) and the U.S. Department of Agriculture.

Bamboo belongs to the grass family, Gramineae, tribe Bambuseae, and is distinguished by the special structure of its stem or culm, the fact that it reaches full height in a short period, its rapid rate of growth, and its singular flowering habits.

Elvin McDonald is a well-known author, photographer, and garden columnist who is an expert plantsman. He is the director of special projects at the Brooklyn Botanic Garden.

A Phyllostachys *species grows close to the entrance of this Japanese Garden. The fence itself is made of bamboo some of which is split.*

The characteristics of bamboo demand the use of two special words. "Culm" is used in place of trunk, which fits trees well enough but is inappropriate here since the culm grows so rapidly, has joints, and is hollow. Similarly, the generic "root" uneasily suits bamboo. Bamboo has indeed a very large growth below ground and also small roots prosper, but what distinguishes it—or at least many species—is the rhizome. This is a long and fast-growing underground shoot from which grow the new sprouts. It is the speed with which the rhizome travels underground that accounts for the spacing of the culms, each of which possesses its own system of small roots.

There are two main types of growth. Bamboo is found either in clumps of culms or as single, free-standing culm. Those marked "clumper" or "sympodial" are well-behaved. Those marked "runner" or "monopodial" can be invasive. In a grove the amount of rhizome intersection is formidable and this is the reason why such a subterranean network holds the ground so firmly. Each joint or node of this far-spreading rhizome bears a single bud yearly and some of these germinate to grow through the surface and become new bamboo. These single sprouts already possess in emerging the final diameter of the adult culm. The culms are erect and are clean of branches for a considerable height.

In all types of bamboo, the most striking characteristic is immense vitality. Bamboo, it seems, can overcome almost any kind of hardship. With its far-ranging network of growth beneath the ground, all shoots are linked and nourish each other and propagate apparently without end. A grove at Hiroshima in 1945 at ground zero survived the atomic blast and within days sent up new shoots.

The speed of bamboo's growth is one of the wonders of nature. Koichiro Ueda, a Japanese authority, has reported one bamboo plant grew 47.6 inches in 24 hours. From the time when a sprout first comes through the ground to the completion of its growing, only about 60 days elapse. After this period, the bamboo culm does little; it gains no height, does not thicken, and it undergoes only slight change. It is alive, of course, indeed flourishing, and seeks sustenance avidly—though not for itself but to provide food for the sprouts that succeed it and for the network of rhizomes and young culms that constitute its family.

The vigor and fertility of bamboo is also remarkable. Every year there appear shoots in great numbers, which in turn produce more, and so it spreads until checked or disciplined by the gardener. Bamboo propagates by the branching of its underground rhizomes and does this asexually.

Even in the same planting there can be a difference of up to two months in the times in which sprouts appear from the soil. Generally, the earlier sprouts are best, developing into larger culms of higher quality. The main season for growth is spring to early summer. The age of the rhizome is relevant to which buds germinate. The three- to five-year rhizomes are the most fertile in producing new culms, while sprouts are rare from rhizomes older than age ten.

Bamboo culms grown in the same year and in the same planting differ in size. Mostly the large-size culms develop from the thicker, younger rhizomes. But even the sizes of the culms from the same rhizome can vary, depending on the amount of nutrients in the soil.

The culm grows so rapidly that it has no time to provide sustenance for itself and therefore growth is entirely dependent on nourishment received through the rhizome and the parent bamboo. The number of new culms in a grove

Water flows through a length of dry bamboo falling into a stone basin. This Japanese garden is in Portland, Oregon.

fluctuates yearly; normally, a good year alternates with one of lower production, although this can be controlled to some extent by fertilizing.

The leaves of bamboo fall yearly, but they give place at once to new ones. The monopodial or running species change foliage in spring, the sympodial or clumping species shed theirs in winter. Bamboo, like any other plant, gains much nutrition from its leaves. Those species

with a larger leaf area absorb more water and grow with more vigor.

When the conditions of the environment become less than favorable, the bamboo seeks security by developing larger leaves. This is especially noticeable after the rare flowering of bamboo, when the small regenerated shoots that do appear bear for a long while leaves which are unusually large.

Cultivation in the Garden

When bamboo is young, leave it uncut. This will encourage strong shoots to sprout every year

and will enhance the quality of leaves. However, selectively thin the older culms every autumn. They are easily damaged by insects, and they also inhibit new shoots. Cut the large-culmed plants when they reach age five or six, the smaller culms at age three or four.

When the older bamboos are allowed to remain, the number of new plants is reduced, but these will in turn tend to be larger in diameter.

Severe pruning of individual bamboo culms is, unlike the pruning of other plants, discouraging to their growth and beauty. Bamboo may be pruned at its top in moderation; do this when

27

growth of the shoot is nearly complete and when one or two branches are beginning to appear from the lower part of the culm. Once done, a profusion of fresh leaves will grow in the following year.

To produce culms of larger diameter, leave the largest culms uncut since it is their characteristics that are transmitted to the next generation. In selecting culms to produce those of the largest growth, it is common sense also to excise the small or the unhealthy bamboo. Fertilization is essential to promote the healthiest growth and an increase in diameter.

Planting Bamboo

Bamboo is so versatile it can grow in almost any natural lighted area, from full sun to partial shade. Bamboo can be transported at any time of year by careful treatment. However, the best months for planting are autumn, early winter and early spring. Replant as quickly as possible to prevent rootlets from drying.

After transplanting, bamboo needs daily watering to the point of saturation for ten days, then on a regular schedule to maintain a moist soil. These plants are constantly in need of water and require a plentiful supply all year. But they also need to be in a well-drained situation—nothing swampy—whether in the ground outdoors or in containers inside.

While you're watering bamboos, they'll revel in a good misting to moisten the leaves and also to remove any dust that may have accumulated. This is of special importance to those grown indoors.

Bamboos do best in well-drained, light, sandy soil. Soil that is too dense and doesn't allow water to drain properly is a chief cause of failure. Indoors fresh air that circulates freely is a must.

The quality and yield of bamboo is much improved by fertilization. The culms become bigger and the healthiest dark green leaves appear. Bamboo consumes a considerable amount of inorganic nutrients, which are supplied in the normal course through the soil or by rain. But under intensive cultivation, not enough are naturally available and supplements are necessary.

Constant watering can deplete the soil of nutrients. Bamboos need an acid soil, pH 6.5 to 6.8. During the active growth period when new shoots are growing and leafing out, they can be fertilized as often as weekly. Nitrogen is the element most needed, followed by potassium, phosphorus and silica. Experiments show the most effective proportions for application are nine to ten parts nitrogen, five parts phosphorus, five parts potassium and six parts silica. The ideal quantity is about one pound of nitrogen per 100 square feet, with the other elements in proportion.

When a concentrated fertilizer is used, apply in earliest spring or a month before the sprouts are expected to appear above ground, and again in early summer before the best growing season of the rhizome. A balanced slow-release fertilizer such as Osmocote 18-6-12 or equivalent may be used.

When grown outdoors, bamboos go into dormancy or a resting period from autumn through winter. These times vary, depending on the area and severity of cold. *Bambusa* has a longer dormancy than other genera, lasting until the weather is dependably warm and settled.

Indoors, however, the dormancy diminishes and, in some cases, all but disappears. Some tropical species actually do better in an indoor environment.

When a bamboo is dormant it stops or slows external growth. Many of the indoor species will not go into dormancy but they will still periodically shed foliage. When this happens, throw the leaves back on the top of the soil. They add an interesting effect and provide the plant with a source of silica, an element beneficial to the plant's growth. These dead leaves form the best type of mulch. Enough of them can even decrease the amount of fertilizer needed. Conversely, an overabundance of falling leaves may be a sign of soil dryness, so be sure to keep bamboo roots properly moistened.

Phyllostachys nigra, *black bamboo, grows along a fence in this Japanese garden. This bamboo does not require as much water as some.*

28

Controlling Running Bamboo

Running bamboo spreads rapidly. Its growth must be restricted or it will soon form a thick jungle that extends many feet beyond the original planting.

A curb made of sheet metal, concrete or asbestos board will prevent bamboo from spreading. A ditching machine can be used to cut a narrow ditch around the grove and the barrier poured or built into the ditch. The curb must surround the planting. The top of the curb should be about one inch above the soil surface, and the curb should extend 24 to 30 inches into the ground. Any joints in the curb must be lapped and secured tightly; bamboo rhizomes can force their way through very small openings.

Buildings, wide driveways, and roads also restrict the spread of bamboo. If the bamboo is planted in a turf area, mowing will destroy unwanted canes by cutting them while they are still small and soft.

Unless the planting is curbed, rhizomes of a running bamboo will spread beyond the edge of the grove a distance approximately equal to the height of the canes. If you plan to grow bamboo

without curbs, be careful in choosing a planting site; protect yourself and your neighbor from unwanted bamboo in flower beds, hedges, and shrubbery plantings.

Bamboo Shoots for Food

The *Phyllostachys* species produce edible shoots. After shoots to be eaten begin to emerge from the soil, dig immediately. Use a narrow

Pleioblastus variegatus, *dwarf white-stripe bamboo, is a running-type of bamboo so must be contained in order to prevent spreading.*

spade and push straight down into the soil on all sides of the shoot. When it is severed from the rhizome and the soil is loosened, pull the shoot from the soil.

Remove the sheaths from the bamboo shoot. First, cut off the bottom or approximately one-third of the shoot. Next pull off with the fingers the outer, tougher sheaths. Then cut off the tender inner sheaths above the growing point of the shoots and peel off.

The shoots of *Phyllostachys dulcis* have no bitter taste. All others should be boiled at least five minutes and the water discarded before they are cooked further or mixed with other foods.

Bamboo for Interiorscaping

Source: *INTERIORSCAPE* magazine, July/August 1987

Sources

Field-grown *Phyllostachys nigra* 'Henon,' a tall, green cane type has been widely employed, often provided by Thomas Brothers, Cameron, N.C.

More recently, Florida growers have organized to produce a variety of bamboos for this market: *Bambusa tuldoides* and *Bambusa glaucescens* (fernleaf) from Tornello Nursery, Ruskin, FL; *Phyllostachys dulcis* and *Arundinaria sastuosa* from Naranja Nursery, Miami, FL. Also, from Hawaii, *Bambusa vulgaris* 'Vittata'.

One view is that the clumpers are better for interiorscaping because they won't invade open areas or girdle themselves into decline when containerized. Another view is that runners are better because northern genera such as *Phyllostachys* come from dry air, cool climates and require less water. The tropical clumpers are accustomed to high humidity and lots of water.

Designers' View

Bamboo serves a unique purpose for height (often in narrow space) and airy, willowy, non-tree appearance. The Hawaiian has large caliper canes with variegation, the potential for towering effect—but expensive. The domestic gives overall airy, lacy appearance and is relatively inexpensive.

Cultural Needs

Light: 800-2000 footcandles ideal; tolerant of light levels as low as 50-75 fc. *Bambusa* has proven itself at 125-400 fc for days of eight to nine hours duration. (Ficus trees tend to shade themselves out. The mantle of new leaves shades out the older ones so they fall off. Bamboo does not do this and thus tolerates less light than might be expected.)

Soil: Sandy, organic loam, well-drained. Ideal pH: 6.5-6.8. No more than 10 percent peat moss. High percent of leaf mold, supplemented with sand or soil. If not leaf mold, use odor-treated cow manure to add organisms that help break down nutrients in the soil. Soilless mix is not recommended.

Water Needs: Water freely. Avoid extreme drying (provokes leaf drop) and never leave standing in water.

Fertilizer: Time-release such as Sierra Osmocote 18-6-12, supplemented with liquid fertilizer every 45-60 days. A well-drained situation is mandatory, however, to avoid salt build up. Do not use a blossom-inducing NPK such as 15-30-15 or 1-6-5.

Miscellaneous Tips

- Containerized stock is preferable in situations where the indoor garden must look ship-shape from the day of installation. Field-grown transplants go through a period of shock and recuperation before they are presentable.
- Emerging rhizomes should not be touched. They are as vulnerable as that of asparagus and will also readily snap or break if disturbed.

A woven bamboo fence provides a screen and textural interest in a west coast garden.

The American Bamboo Society (1101 San Leon Ct., Solana Beach, CA 92075) annually produces a source list of bamboo plants, available free to any gardener who requests it and sends a long, self-addressed, stamped envelope.

Bamboos in Flower

David McClintock

In April of 1983, I published a note in *The Garden* on the flowering of the Himalayan *Arudinaria jaunsarensis* (as we must now call *A. anceps*). The response has shown that more can usefully be recorded about this phenomenon. For phenomenon it is. What brings a bamboo into flowering condition remains mysterious. The statement that the plants of a given species will all flower in the same year and then die, has been known for many years to be far from trustworthy, at least for nearly all the sorts we grow in England. Yet I hear it being repeated constantly.

I write "nearly all," because one species, the lovely *Thamnocalamus (Arundinaria) falconeri,* does seem to have a blooming cycle of roughly 30 years—never exactly the same—and when the bout has finished, all the plants die, mercifully leaving some seedlings. But in no other species can I detect such a clear interval between flowerings.

One difficulty is defining what is meant by flowering. It can occur as a single floret buried in a mass of leaves; it can occur on only one culm of a clump, or on only one clump of several; it can cover all the clumps in an area with flowers, or it may do this in every area everywhere, full gregarious flowering—the rarest form, at least in Europe. Furthermore the same plant can go on flowering, often quite profusely, for decades, with stamens appearing in suitable weather every month of the year.

Bamboos are members of the grass family and many kinds are used in gardens for their decorative effect. But bamboos also have a mystique about their flowering habits, especially when one hears of Chinese pandas suffering when entire groves perish after producing blossoms. Mr. McClintock discusses bamboo flowering based on his experiences in England. —P.L.

Even with full flowering, it remains rare, in my experience, for a plant to die. While its strength goes into producing flowers, the leaves starve, shrivel, drop off, and photosynthesis slows down or ceases. But there is goodness stored in the rhizomes of well-established plants. Sooner or later the weakening bout will lose its force, and fresh shoots will reassert themselves, often starting with just one green leaf low down.

Meanwhile the plant will look awful, and many gardeners will decide that it was on the way out and dispose of it. If it had been left, it would most likely have recovered. I have seen this happen many times in many species.

Arundinaria simonii *var.* variegata *(left)*
A. viridistriata *(right)*
Bamboos are members of the grass family and many can be used decoratively along with other grasses. Use with caution because some can be invasive.

David McClintock is an English plantsman who writes and lectures extensively on the bamboos. He wrote about the bamboo family for the European Garden Flora *and his articles have appeared in* The Garden, The Plantsman, Amateur Gardening, *and the publications of the various bamboo societies.*

It is true that occasionally plants die following the debilitating effects of flowering. But this has usually been brought on by some other factor operating on the weakened plant such as extreme weather, or the plant being in an unsuitable site or not having had time to settle in—a big bamboo may need three years or more to get established in new quarters.

Seed is by no means always produced outside a plant's native area, or if it is, may not germinate. When any is found, it should always be sown fresh. The special importance of seed is the light that seedlings can throw on relationships of the plants we grow; we can classify beyond vegetative features. Varieties with variegated leaves rarely, if ever, produce variegated seedlings, but revert to their all-green progenitor—which sometimes leads to name complications.

Once a species starts to flower, nothing will stop it. If it is really full flowering, other plants of the same species may be expected to follow suit, and up to five years or more later, flower.

It may help to exemplify these general remarks with comments on some of the species on which flowering has been seen in the last year or so.

Arundinaria jaunsarensis has had flowers on this attractive, if invasive, bamboo for 25 years, never a year without. Furthermore there are clumps where I could find flowers, often plenty, year after year for as long as 20 years, and still do! During the past two years however, flowering has been on a much greater scale, but even so, there are still sterile clumps. Some of these may be seedlings from the early days of flowering, and it remains to be seen what sort of flowering pattern they may show. Seed production has been variable, mostly none at all, but sometimes quite plentiful and fertile.

Indocalamus (Sasa) tessellatus is an Indian species, floppy in habit because it has the longest, largest leaves of any bamboo on thin stalks. This used to be a standard example of a plant which never flowered. Nor has it anywhere, to my knowledge, except California from 1979 to 1982. But once our plants had good flowers, its stamens could be counted to determine in which genus it belonged—it has three, whereas *Sasa* has six. So flowering made accurate classification possible, and changed the generic name.

Pleioblastus chino is a relatively ordinary bamboo, up to seven feet tall with medium-size leaves, and it runs. It has been an overlooked species, given various other names until recently, but is not rare. I have flowering specimens for one or another variety for 1966-67 and since 1979. But this seems to have been only spasmodic, often the leaves hardly suffering and, at least once, massive flowering on one culm in one clump in one year and never any more since. Seed has been variably produced, sometimes in quantity, and has germinated well.

Pleioblastus variegatus (Arundinaria fortunei and *A. variegata* in *Hortus Third)* is a nice plant with two forms at least; one gets up to three feet, the other stays half that size. Both started to flower in a small way in 1976, and are slowly spreading, but many clumps remain sterile. The leaves are narrow, dark green with white stripes, but the seeds will produce only green-leaved plants. They are still *P. variegatus,* but differentiated as var. *viridis.* In addition to the present bout, this species flowered 15 years earlier in Copenhagen; the seedlings were also all green.

Pleioblastus viridi-striatus (Arundinaria auricoma and *A. viridistriata* in *Hortus Third)* is even lovelier with broad golden yellow leaves and pale green stripes, growing to five feet in height. Its leaves look best if the stems are cut down early in the year, but if they are not, solitary spikelets may be found on top of some of the stems, without the leaves being affected in any way at all. I have yet to find seed to prove its postulated green origin.

Phyllostachys species can readily be identified by culms having a marked groove between alternate nodes, where there are two unequal branches with sometimes a thin third one between them, these similarly grooved. None of the species most frequently grown seem to be flowering here at the moment, but one more commonly grown on the continent can be seen in the bamboo garden at Kew, *P. aureosulcata.* It has, as its name denotes, a yellow groove on its rough greenish culms and *P. nuda* has also started to flower there (*nuda* from having no bristles on its sheaths). Other species should soon flower if there is anything to their claimed cycles. *P. aurea* in particular is "overdue," as was reported to me from Sweden in 1982. I have heard of no more, but have a seedling germinated from their seed. That species has a cup-shaped swelling beneath each node.

Pseudosasa (Arundinaria) japonica must be our most common bamboo, surviving maltreatment and neglect. But even when it is well grown, it is no more than "Yet another bamboo"—well, that is my opinion, and I have groves of it! In my poor sandy soil it can exceed 12 feet, and normally stays in tight clumps with only an occasional wandering rhizome. Five years ago I called its flowering "scrappy, irregular and unpredictable," and so it seemed. But after I wrote in *The Garden,* the majority of specimens sent me were of this species and not *A. jaunsarensis.* These are probably our two most frequently grown species, and it so happens that both have been flowering for two decades or more in varying degree, but profusely in the past two years or so. Even so, not all clumps have flowered.

Sasa kurilensis is another bamboo more common abroad than in England. There are two forms under this name, one a dwarf of not more than eight inches, the other up to eight feet. (Editor's note: the dwarf turns out to be *Pseudosasa owatarii.*) Both have been flowering quite generally since 1979. This is another dullard, the small one like the neater *Pleioblastus (Arundinaria) pygmaeus* (on which no flowering has lately been noted, another value of flowering records). The taller rather resembles *Pseudosasa japonica.*

Sasa palmata is a fearsome runner, some-times six feet a year. But where it can be contained or accommodated, it is worth it for its superb large, very broad (up to four inches) leaves, bright green for 12 months of the year, atop six-foot stems. It has flowered endlessly from 1961, and still has not finished. Seed is rarely produced and the only germination I have come across was a self-sown seedling.

Sasella ramosa (Arundinaria vagans) is another rampant species, three- to four-feet high with a single wide branch at each node, and leaves that may get a narrow dead edge in hard English winters. Forms of this had been known to flower in its native Japan, but never anywhere else. Then suddenly in 1981 a single patch at Kew burst into full flower and produced seeds (but I have yet to hear of germination). This particular patch lost its flowers after two years, but flowering spread to other patches, and has since been noted in widely separated places—on the continent too—but there are still many flowerless patches. There is no sign of the plants completely dying, despite the vigor of their flowering.

Semiarundinaria (Arundinaria) fastuosa forms towering clumps with a bunch of short branches at each node. It has been flowering since at least 1957. I watched the same clumps flowering incessantly year after year for over 20 years. During that time many gardeners lost patience and grubbed them up. Those that did not now have 12-foot culms in full figure. Even so, there were flowers still in 1983 at Kew, but never a seed anywhere.

Herein I mention only the most frequent or relevant species that may be seen in flower at the time of this writing in 1984—of which there are some half dozen more at least. There are also about a dozen which so far have never flowered here; one or two have never been known to flower anywhere. Only when we have accumulated much more data —the most valuable coming from observations of the same clump over many years— may we be able to realize what causes bamboos to flower. ━◣

Ornamental Grasses

Molina caerulea *'Variegata', purple moor grass,
is a blue grass and is clump forming. The flowers
are borne in arching sprays and are purple.*

3

2

1

0

Grasses to the horizon moving like a sea in the wind are far from the decorative clumps found in garden borders. But between the giant bamboos that grow ten feet a season and the dwarfs of our lawns, there are grasses whose effects in well-considered combination with other plants, are as beautiful as a meadow.

Pamela Harper

During the last five years there has been a surge of interest in ornamental grasses. The landscape architects Oehme, van Sweden & Associates of Washington, D.C. have had a lot to do with this. They have demonstrated how beautiful grasses can be, not only in private gardens, but in such conspicuous public places as the parklike area around the Federal Reserve Building in Washington. Some of the thousands of visitors to the nation's capital will certainly have gone home with new ideas for their own gardens. A frustrating search for the plants may have followed but the situation is improving, though demand still often exceeds supply. Making a choice among over a hundred listed grasses might now be the problem. Many are new to me, especially the prairie grasses. One little gem among these is mosquito grass, with tiny pink and white combs of flowers held obliquely to the stalks and seeming to hover; a curiosity for the rock garden. Other than this I'll confine myself to familiar grasses, using the term loosely to include a few sedges, reeds and rushes.

Many annual and tender perennial grasses are grown for their inflorescences, to be

Pamela Harper is the owner of the Harper Horticultural Slide Library and one of the premier garden and plant photographers of the garden world. Her book, The Story of a Garden, *chronicles the creation and development of a garden by Mrs. Harper and her husband Patrick over a period of sixteen years. She is the co-author of* Perennials, How to Select, Grow, and Enjoy.

admired on the plant or dried in bouquets. Seed catalogs illustrate quite a lot, with such evocative names as animated oats, cloud grass, golden-top, bridal-veil and ornamental corn. Quaking grass, *Briza maxima,* has been grown by generations of gardeners for its panicles of pendant lockets quivering on wire-fine stalks. This is an annual, and so is the scaled down *B. minor,* but *B. media*—also known as trembling grass, shakers and doddering-dickies—is a hardy perennial, about 18 inches high, deciduous, but almost evergreen in mild areas. At the front of a flower border its trembling fat spikelets, green fading to beige, add a light touch to the brighter colors.

Fountain grass well describes the four-foot flowering clumps of *Pennisetum setaceum (P. ruppelii),* variable in color but rosy pink in the preferred form, sometimes grown as an annual. Where frost is infrequent it is perennial, as in California, where it is frequently planted, but clumps may rot in winter in wet soil. No sun seems too hot for this drought-resistant grass, but wind can leave it very battered. It is a pest if plumes are not cut before the seeds fall, but the dark-flowered, dark-leaved *P. setaceum* 'Cupreum' is said not to set seed although this needs to be confirmed in California. Excessive self-seeding seldom occurs in colder areas, where the dead plumes of this and the hardier, but less colorful *P. alopecuroides* are left for winter interest.

Bamboos

I could say much about bamboos, and little of it polite. Several proverbs apply: "give them an inch and they'll take a yard," "once bitten, twice shy." Bamboo must have caused more friction between neighbors than any other plants because the taller ones seem so suitable for boundary screens; unfortunately, stoloniferous bamboos recognize no boundaries, and most of the clump-forming kinds are rather tender. If I did feel inclined to try a hair of the dog, it would be with *Chusquea culeou* or *Arundinaria viridistriata*. *Chusquea culeou* is Chilean and Chilean plants are noted for two things: their beauty, and their poor adaptability to other climates. So it would be a gamble, but one worth taking in mild climates where it could be given moderately moist, fertile soil and shelter from wind. Plumelike stems of slender, two-inch deep green leaves comprise the dense, ferny, slightly vase-shaped, exceptionally graceful non-invasive clumps, seldom more than eight feet high though capable to twice as much. Unlike most bamboos, the canes are solid and the leaves do not wilt when stems are cut. Mature canes are clad to the base with short leafy branches but first year canes are bare, very dark green and punctuated with conspicuous white sheaths from the nodes.

The other bamboo that tempts me from time to time is hardier but less restrained, and I've seen it escape too often to put my trust in bottomless tubs or flue pipes sunk in the ground, let alone the old tires sometimes entrusted with the job of containing it. *Arundinaria viridistriata* seldom grows as much as waist high. An earlier species name, *A. auricoma* (having golden hair) was apt, because the effect is of a vividly yellow plant, and young leaves are velvety. Look closer and you find that the spear-shaped mature leaves vary: yellow; pale green; yellow flushed green; green flushed yellow; or yellow with green pencil-striping. Raised containers, or beds surrounded by paving set on a concrete slab will keep it in its allotted spot. The color is brightest in full sun which may, however, scorch or curl the leaves, especially if the soil is dry. Each gardener must experiment to find the best place. Hard frost kills the leaves, but they stay on the plant—shantung colored and with a silky sheen when struck by the low rays of the sun.

For those averse to yellow foliage, there's a white and green counterpart in *Arundinaria variegata.* For more about bamboos, turn to *New Western Garden Book,* where thirty-six are described.

Pampas grass

Cortaderia selloana is too imposing to be a good mixer and most fittingly stands alone in grass or paving. Where hardy it is easy to grow, even below high tideline on the beach. In California care must be taken in planting pampas grass to be sure that *C. selloana* is used and not *C. jubata,* which is an invasive pest throughout the state. For gardeners deprived of this because winter lows fall regularly below 10°F, there's an equally impressive substitute in *Erianthus ravennae.* Less bushy but loftier plumes, rearing up 10 feet or more, have the spun-glass lucency of a squirrel's tail against the light. The foxy brown winter color is also very appealing—all in all an under-appreciated plant for fertile, moist but well-drained soil, hardy well below zero, though with the risk that the flowering plumes may be damaged by early autumn frost.

My resolve never again to grow pampas grass, after cutting myself on the saw-edged leaves while trying to hack a clump apart, weakened at sight of the cultivar 'Gold Band' combined with gray artemisia and blue agapanthus, the prettiest association seen during a three-week gardens tour. The name misleads, it is striped, not banded. I bought it, it died, and its place has been filled by *Miscanthus sinensis* 'Zebrinus', which really is gold-banded. There are hundreds of plants with vertical striping but very few with horizontal

Oehme, van Sweden & Associates have designed many gardens using a combination of grasses, perennials and woody plants. This one in Minnesota has only grasses.

bars, which go "against the grain" so to speak. In the moist (even wet) soil preferred by these plants, 'Zebrinus' stands shoulder high, topped through autumn and winter with feathery plumes. *M. sinensis* 'Strictus', called porcupine grass, is similar but shorter, narrower and more upright. At least a dozen other cultivars are obtainable, of which 'Gracillimus', a four-foot fountain of narrow ribbons, and white-striped 'Variegatus' are easiest to find and among the best. When to divide or transplant grasses depends on where you live. Transplanting should, ideally, be followed by the longest possible period without excessive

cold, heat, drought, wind or rain, but the ideal must sometimes yield to expediency. In prying off a chunk of 'Zebrinus' I broke a fork and nearly my back, so anyone much over forty years of age might do well to tackle the job whenever they happen to have a strong man with saw, mattock and axe. If in doubt about the plant's survival leave part of the clump where it is as insurance.

Hakonechloa macra 'Albo-variegata' comes from Japan and is a winner. It appears in catalogs under different cultivar names, but they all are the same.

Reeds

Two impressive grasses of somewhat similar appearance are the giant reeds, *Phragmites australis (P. communis)* and *Arundo donax,* wetland plants invaluable for beautifying low-lying wasteland, as phragmites does long stretches of East Coast interstates. Both have Jekyll and Hyde characteristics, being extremely invasive in wet soils but quite likely to die in dry ones. Of several cultivars, only *Arundo donax* 'Versicolor' seems to be available; this is reminiscent of sweet corn but with each leaf striped in cream and green broadly margined with white. It is cold-tender (more so than other plants of the species), vagrant, and the leaves may scorch in dry climates, but effort to overcome these shortcomings as best you may is well worthwhile for this showiest of all variegated grasses.

If a plant is attractive, fairly easy to grow, and not too difficult to propagate, it is well on the road to popularity, but not necessarily universal popularity. Having met those requirements, a less obvious factor comes into play, one I became aware of on moving from England to the southeastern United States and found that yellow foliage had lost some of its appeal; the psychological effect is different under sunny skies. On the East Coast many grasses, wild and cultivated, are most appealing in autumn and early winter. As the year explodes in a climax of brilliance from the trees, the dead stems and leaves of deciduous grasses have the same tawny gleam as the sunlit coat of a golden retriever, while the plumed or hazy inflorescences assume a radiance in the Indian-summer sunshine unexcelled by any other plant. Deciduous grasses favored by Oehme, van Sweden & Associates for this effect include the three foot vertical clumps of *Calamagrostis* ('Karl Foerster' is a particularly fine cultivar), arching *Pennisetum alopecuroides,* and *Miscanthus sinensis* 'Gracillimus' with its slender weeping leaves and feather-duster plumes. By combining these with evergreens such as yuccas and mugo pine, foreground ground covers such as epimediums and bergenias, and perennials that stay long in bloom and remain attractive when dead, especially *Sedum* 'Autumn Joy' and *Rudbeckia fulgida,* a picture is created that changes with the seasons and never lacks interest. Sometimes the grasses are massed, sometimes well spaced among rocks and gravel. The grasses remain effective through most of winter and are never more appreciated than when rising above a sparkling carpet of snow.

But what of regions where summers are dry, winters mild, and rainy autumn heralds not a winding down but a resurgence of growth? Might green better suit the mood of this new growing season? In any event, dead brown grasses are seen at their best where autumn is sunny and comparatively dry; under persistently gray skies they may look drab and rainbedraggled. There are evergreen sedges from New Zealand (*Carex buchananii* is one) which are always brown or copper colored; might these be in keeping where brown is the characteristic color of the summer landscape, or would they seem to have died of drought? I'd need to live there to know. These coppery sedges are uncommon and names are confused: *Carex buchananii* should be V-shaped, but a grass of weeping habit (equally desirable) sometimes bears this name.

Most of the reeds and rushes and some of the sedges need or prefer marshy soil or shallow water, and so do a few of the grasses, but those mentioned next will also grow in soil only moderately moist. *Acorus gramineus* 'Variegatus' (an Aroid) makes gappy foot-high clumps of sword-shaped leaves grouped in narrow fans. Roughly half the quarter-inch width of each leaf is green, the other half cream; it looks more at home in a manicured setting than a naturalistic one and never better than when growing through pebbles in a pot.

Umbrella-plant, *Cyperus alternifolius,* makes a good pot plant for those who find it hard to gauge the right amount of water. Overwatering is almost impossible, and underwatering can be guarded against by standing the pot in a water-filled outer container. In summer, or year round in warm climates, it can be plunged in a garden pool or grown in a moist border. An elderly lady told me she got new plants by cutting off the "umbrellas" and putting them upside down in shallow water (hers were in the bird bath). I was sceptical, but tried it, and found she was right. It is killed at 20 °F , as are most of its kith and kin but not, unfortunately, that beautiful but pestiferous weed, *Cyperus esculentus* or nut grass, seed of which is sometimes offered for sale; avoid it like the plague.

Variegation
Bowles' golden sedge might be found under *Carex stricta* 'Aurea', *C. riparia* 'Bowles', or *Carex elata* 'Bowles' Golden'— they are all the same thing, and a lovely thing it is, with slender flexed leaves about two feet long, seemingly pure golden yellow though actually thinly margined green. The color is brightest in full sun, and wet soil alongside a pond or stream is the perfect spot for it. It isn't a beginner's plant, being often difficult to establish. Don't confuse it with Bowles' golden grass, *Milium effusum* 'Aureum', a graceful yellow-leaved wood-millet, easily grown from seed, and a cheerful plant for heavy, moist soil in partial shade.

Three rather similar, winter-dormant wetland grasses grown for their striped ribbon-like arching leaves are: *Glyceria maxima (G. aquatica)* 'Variegata', or manna grass, about four feet high with leaves striped cream; *Phalaris arundinacea* var. *picta*—the ribbon grass or gardeners' garters, of similar height with leaves striped white; and the taller *Spartina pectinata* 'Aureo-marginata' with leaves striped yellow. Assessed solely on appearance, my own first choice would be glyceria, which is at its best in mud or shallow water. Spartina would be the one for brackish marshes. Phalaris, besides being beautiful, is exceptionally hardy (to about—30 °F.) and will grow in quite dry soil. All three are determined colonizers, phalaris less so in dry soil but it still needs watching. *P. arundinacea* 'Feesey's Form' is said to be superior and non-invasive, and 'Dwarf's Garters' is a shorter, twelve-inch, variegated cultivar.

Gray and Blue
Now a group grown mainly for the appeal of their living leaves, though most also have attractive flowers. Trying not to play dog-in-the-manger, I'll put the blue ones first. On acid seashore sand in Virginia these are among my failures; humid heat and high rainfall is probably what upsets them, as it does a lot of gray-leaved plants.

Most gardeners know blue fescue, usually sold as *Festuca glauca. Hortus Third* calls it *F. ovina* var. *glauca*. In his recent book, *Ornamental Grasses,* Roger Grounds calls it *F. caesia*. Kurt Bluemel calls it *F. cinerea* 'Superba' and lists also the cultivar 'Blausilber'. Under whatever name, blue fescue makes pattable cushions of soft, needle-fine blades six to eight inches high, not good for massing because the tuffets maintain their individual rounded shape and insinuate themselves into the gaps. Crowded clumps may rot, and even well-spaced ones get shabby if not divided every year or two. *F. amethystina* is a similar but taller plant of 18 inches or so.

Of similar color, but taller and of firmer outline, *Helictotrichon sempervirens (Avena sempervirens)* seems to demand a formal setting—perhaps a single plant in paving, or a group of three well-spaced clumps growing through a ground cover of pebbles. Slender spiky leaves grow upright at the center of the clump, those at the edges are arching. When topped with stalks of loosely clustered grayish flowers the plants reach four feet in height. Sandy soil in sun is said to be their preference. Metallic blue and broader bladed, plants of *Elymus arenarius* are of more relaxed mein—rather untidy in fact. Though lauded by no less a personage than Gertrude Jekyll, I'd hesitate to admit to my garden a plant of such incurable exuberance. It is a seashore plant, sometimes used for stablizing dunes, but the handsomest planting I've seen was in wet, heavy clay; which only shows that you can't always go by the book.

The only blue thing about *Molinia caerulea* 'Variegata' is the name. The flowers are sometimes purplish and purple moor grass is one popular name. There's gentleness about

Molina caerulea 'Variegata' has arching leaves, creamy striping and brownish or purplish flowers on cream stalks. It is even attractive at the end of the season as it begins to turn brown. It is clump forming.

this plant, the leaves limply arching, the creamy striping merging with cream stalks holding aloft slightly arching sprays of brownish or purplish flowers to a height of two feet or so. It is clump forming, blends with almost everything, does well in sun or part shade and adapts to most soils not excessively wet, dry or alkaline. It is hardy at 25 °F but the leaves turn brown with the first frosts.

Yellow

Hakonechloa, from Japan, is a winner. Plants of *Hakonechloa macra,* with green leaves are not being sold, though they are in cultivation. Three cultivar names appear in literature but all the plants I've seen have been the same. White Flower Farm (Litchfield, Connecticut 06759) claims to have introduced it to the United States and they give it the name *H. macra* 'Albo-aurea Variegata'. It is the same plant as *H. macra* 'Aureola' of English gardens. Moist, humus-rich acid soil suits it best, with shade from direct sun where summers are hot. Slowly spreading clumps combine dramatic color with delicate texture and graceful form. They look yellow, but

45

each slender tapering blade is pencilled with green and sometimes flushed pink or bronze. It is flowerless so far and there seems to be doubt about whether it belongs with the grasses or the bamboos. *Alopecurus pratensis* 'Aureo-variegatus' has similarly brilliant coloring on a denser, more upright plant, scarcely 18 inches high with cylindrical clusters of flowers held well above the foliage. Grow this in full sun or part shade, in fertile well-drained soil. Clumps spread moderately fast but an infestation need not be feared.

Variegated bulbous oat grass, *Arrhenatherum elatius* 'Bulbosum Variegatum' is easily recognizable, if you dig a bit up, by the chain of maize-shaped basal nodes, each capable of making a new plant. This is one of the prettiest grasses, with clean white striping and dainty flowers. In my garden it tries to go summer dormant, doesn't quite manage it and hangs about looking shabby. It smartens itself up for a couple of months in autumn and then goes dormant with the coming of cold weather. It may behave differently in other climates.

Problems

Finally—though not because the topic is exhausted, I've barely scratched the surface —two current favorites. Attempts to unravel the tangled names of these two somewhat similar sedges have met with only partial success. They resemble each other in size and habit: in moist leaf mold and partial shade fist-sized divisions have made dense clumps 18 inches in diameter after three years. Each slender leaf is over a foot in length, but because they arch or spread sideways, the height of the clumps is little more than eight inches. The tough, once-pleated leaves look glossy and smooth, and they feel that way if you run your fingers from base to tip, but

Pennisetum setaceum *'Burgundy Giant' is combined with* Celosia plumosa *'Century' in Brooklyn Botanic Garden's annual border.*

rubbed the other way they are raspy towards the tip. So much for similarities, now the names and differences. From sundry names thrown into the pot by catalogs, articles, reference books (no two of which quite agree, nor do their descriptions precisely match the plants before my eyes) and learned friends, I have picked the two I think most likely, with other names under which they might be found in parentheses. Both plants are from Japan.

Carex morrowii 'Aurea-Variegata', or 'Aureo-Variegata', or 'Variegata Aurea' *(C. morrowii* var. *expallida, C. morrowii* 'Variegata', *C. morrowii* 'Evergold') has leaves one-quarter inch wide. Sometimes the striation is a bit more complicated but most of the leaves are deep cream in the middle with a fairly narrow dark green edge. The overall effect is a showy creamy yellow in combed clumps from which fallen leaves are easily raked. In my garden this plant does extremely well if given deep, moist soil and some shade from afternoon sun. It is an undamaged evergreen down to 20 °F, is shabby at lower temperatures and perishes at about zero. It is not uncommon, and all seem agreed that it belongs to the species *C. morrowii*.

Carex conica 'Variegata' *(C. morrowii* var. *expallida, C. morrowii* var. *albo marginata, C. morrowii* 'Variegata') has leaves little more than one-eighth inch wide, dark green very narrowly edged with white. The somewhat silvery effect is less dramatic and easier to blend with other plants. Though preferring rich, moist soil and part shade it is more tolerant of sun, drought and poor soil than its counterpart. It is also a great deal hardier, to well below 0 °F for prolonged periods. It is primarily on the basis of this greater hardiness that I have accepted the probability of its being distinct from *C. morrowii,* though doubt remains. Both plants are lovely, singly or in drifts, but the second is the more versatile. I have distributed it as *C. morrowii* 'Variegata' and it is doing well in the gardens of West Coast friends from Seattle to Los Angeles.

Ornamental Grasses of the Southwest High Plains

From the mountains of the Southwest come a different class of ornamental grasses that are more subtle and modest than many of our usual garden grasses.
—P.L.

Gail Haggard

I am writing about a few of the ornamental grasses of the high elevations of the southwest plains, an on-the-dry side, magnificent area of grasslands.

Ornamental has many meanings. If my children play in it, or if I eat it, I consider it to be of the highest ornamental value.

The ancient corns come to mind: blue corn, papago, desert sweet...they are grasses offering ornaments to my plate. Large cobs of gun-metal blue and rainbow corn, and the tiny cobs of strawberry corn, are given at every holiday and birth because of their lasting beauty and as a reminder of our means of sustenance and good fortune. Some of the most intriguing gardens of the Southwest have corn in their ornamental borders—again the huge varieties like papago, or the diminutive like strawberry corn—along with other vegetables and colorful flowers. A well-known Santa Fe restaurant has a narrow bed of corn and sunflowers on the street—it's a landscape delight and a traffic stopper. Maize mazes are a child's delight. When we were little we all played in the corn patch. It was thick and high overhead, a hide-and-seek heaven.

The sweeping ornaments to the eye are either the grasses in the untouched plains,

---

Gail Haggard is the owner of Plants of the Southwest, a marvelous seed house located in Santa Fe, New Mexico, and well-known for its commitment to ecology and the relationships between rocks, plants, earth and weather.

"All flesh is grass."
The Bible

"Grass is the forgiveness of nature—her constant benediction."
John James Ingalls

their more diminutive relatives of the grass meadows, or the native grass lawns. Lawns and meadows in our dry country shouldn't be composed of expensive-to-maintain imports like Kentucky bluegrass (an appropriate beauty to another climate.) The glories of the high plains are the native grama grasses —modest, subtle, but certainly beautiful.

Blue fescue is a familiar grass. It is propagated by division from the bluest form of the native, *Festuca ovina glauca*. It's a blue, perfectly symmetrical hedgehog if trimmed, and if let go to seed, waving open seed heads on stems to four feet appear above the blue base. Try blue fescue in perennial beds, making a checkerboard pattern with soil in between, as an accent in a corner spot or in your rock garden. It is corny and true that a rock is a plant's best friend. The plant can snuggle up to its favorite exposure, get heat in the winter, coolness in the summer, and have the extra water that the rock gives by condensation. A low grass like buffalo grass *(Buchloe dactyloides)* planted between flagstones is another example of this delightful companionship.

Seed-eating birds are attracted to Indian ricegrass. The American Indians collected its seed to grind. The genus, *Oryzopsis* has been a food source worldwide. The seed stalks

Bouteloua gracilis, *blue grama grass, is a native warm-season grass. Its leaf texture makes it a superb alternative lawn grass.*

Drawings by Niki Threlkeld

49

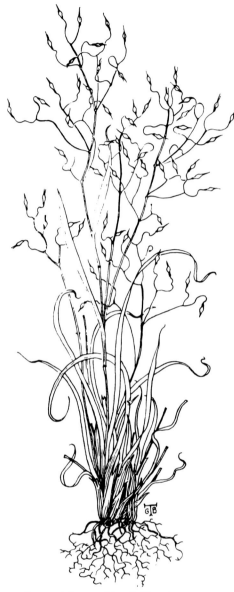

Oryzopsis hymenoides, *Indian ricegrass, grows one- to two-feet tall, prefers sandy soil and is extremely drought resistant.*

make an airy, delicate cloud about the leaves of this bunch grass—beautiful in the meadow, as an accent in the garden, and in dried arrangements. Indian ricegrass *(O. hymenoides)* grows one to two feet tall, prefers sandy soil and is extremely drought resistant.

Little bluestem *(Schizachyrium scoparium)* grows across the Great Plains. Western cattle were driven to its luxurious domain to be fattened up. It's a feast for the eye as well: a tall (three feet here where it's high and dry) bunch grass whose green leaves and stalks turn russet in the fall and look so striking against the snow. The fuzzy seeds that fly to the winds catch the light.

Side-oats grama *(Bouteloua curtipendula)* does not have the leaf texture that makes blue grama *(B. gracilis)* a superb alternative lawn grass, but it surely holds rocky slopes well and, as the name states, the seed is like little oats all lined up on the side of the stalks. Best is the orange-red color of the delicate male part of the flower and, up close, the feathery brush of the female part of the flower—unfortunately only a delight for the close observer.

There is so much more: the blue cast and the strict symmetry of the seed heads of the wheat; the open pattern of alkali sacaton *(Sporobolus airoides)*; the other grass flowers that resemble ocean waves.

The most important category of ornamental grass use is for the lawn—and I hope, more and more, for the meadow. Others have stated their concern more forcibly than I. Charles Mann: "The traditional sod lawn is a conformist nightmare, characteristic of mass mentality, lemming behavior. It is a disaster perpetrated against everyone's best interest by sheep accustomed to "eating" inferior, expensive products."

A local homeowner in our Santa Fe area kept a monthly record of water bills over two years for installation and watering an 8,000-square-foot lawn of Kentucky bluegrass and another of buffalo grass. After installation of the lawns—the bluegrass totaled $6,000 for sod or $4,000 for seed and the buffalo grass was $3,500 for sod or $840 for seed—the maintenance for the bluegrass continued at approximately $415 per year, every year, for water; the buffalo grass cost $150 the first year and nothing after that.

Even if a native lawn were more costly (and that could never be), I'd prefer it. Native grasses are softer with finer leaf blades and are easier to maintain: there is no mowing or edging weekly, no thatching, no fertilizing. It is more disease resistant and if I went on an endless hike, it would be just fine when I returned.

Native grass alternatives such as blue grama or buffalo grass are warm-season grasses. Kentucky bluegrass is a cool-season grass. The warm-season grasses are green while growing during the summer, turning beige and going dormant when it gets cold. Cool-season grasses do their growing in the spring and fall when it is cool. They are dormant in the summer unless they receive a lot of water to keep them actively growing. This is an important visual difference if you move to the Southwest: less green, more beige.

Balls of blue fescue, Festuca ovina glauca, *resemble an army of symmetrical hedgehogs in the bed of ornamental grasses designed by Russell Page for the gardens at Pepsico in New York state.*

A West Coast Garden of Grasses

A California gardener writes about her favorite—and not so favorite—ornamental grasses and how to use them in a garden.
—P.L.

Hermine Stover

That last fateful childhood day in Brooklyn, as I watched an agonized, red-faced man push a lawnmower uphill to level a surface of live green outdoor carpeting, I vowed: "No lawns for me!" But I didn't give up on grasses; on the contrary, I threw myself into collecting and growing ornamental grasses and grasslike plants. I have never mowed a lawn, nor have I lived a day without enjoying the sight of a grass. Those plants which botanists call Gramineae are the true grasses. However, other plants which are grassy in appearance are included here. Some of these are members of the lily and iris families, or other less familiar monocots.

The grasses I grow range in color from carbon paper purple-black to shameless bright pink; from solid color to gaily striped and banded; from tiny plants best appreciated in

Phormum tenax variegatum, *New Zealand flax, is a cousin of agave and has been hybridized and selected into a veritable spectrum of color.*

an equally tiny Japanese pot to massive individuals which take the place of shrubs in the landscape. If I include the bamboos, those woody perennial grasses, I may say that I can garden using plants that vary between tiny tufted ground covers and huge trees, in a rainbow of colors, and still deal only with ornamental grasses.

Grasses and grasslike plants embrace a broad spectrum of climates from swampy, boggy places to arid and rocky locales. The bog plants—which are my personal favorites—include *Acorus,* an aroid which resembles an iris, and comes in solid green, white striped, and in a range of sizes from five to about fifteen inches in height. If you don't have a swamp, you may grow it in a pot kept standing in a saucer of water. Another bog subject, far removed from the true grasses, is the horsetail, *Equisetum hyemale.* This is a jointed, hollow-stemmed fern ally, that attains a height of four feet. It is not a favorite of mine and is perhaps the most invasive plant I know of with a root system equal to reinforced concrete. Wind knocks it over, so plant it in sheltered locations. *E. scirpoides,* a diminutive form, is a delicate thing, almost like a magnified moss. Variegated forms are seen occasionally.

Hermine Stover is co-owner with her husband, Roger, of Endangered Species, a California nursery that specializes in bamboos, ornamental grasses, phormiums, and other unusual offerings in the plant world. Originally from Boston, the Stovers moved to California and pledge they will never become a mega-nursery.

Leaping from the bog to New Zealand, we find the most colorful of the grasslike plants, the *Phormium* genus, commonly called New Zealand flax. This cousin of the agave has been hybridized and selected into a veritable spectrum of color. *Hortus Third* lists "probably two" species *(Phormium colensoi* and *P. tenax)*, but they are available in great numbers ranging from small tufted plants to bushy clumps five feet tall or so. The colors include brilliant rose pink, peach, cream, clay green, a rich and bold maroon, scarlet, orange, yellow, and various striped combinations of all of these colors. They have fanciful cultivar names like 'Maori Maiden', 'Surfrider', 'Dusky Chief', 'Maori Sunrise', 'Sundowner', and 'Dazzler', the last a particular beauty that has magenta leaves striped in chocolate. It is seldom that one sees foliage so brightly colored as to rival flowers, but it is safe to say that the leaf coloring in some phormiums would strike some as gaudy.

Having flung about some of the brightest of colors, I must provide the ultimate in contrast, *Ophiopogon planiscapus nigrescens.* This is a tufted, narrow leafed plant of a color close to the purple black of typing carbonpaper. The bell-shaped flowers are hyacinth in color, and the fruits are translucent and look like amethyst glass beads. It is a member of a larger group of fake grasses which are actually lilies. The green form, *O. japonicus,* is considered a sod-forming plant, but if left to its own devices it will form lumps and humps, and overhang a curb in a way far more interesting than plain old sod. Another species, *O. jaburan,* comes in many kinds of yellow and white striped forms, for which the Japanese have a roster of cultivar names. These however, are grouped together in the United States.

Showy enough for pot culture and perhaps best appreciated that way, is *Imperata cylindrica rubra,* a green grass whose leaf tips are blood red. You don't see that kind of thing often.

Another larger group of true grasses is the genus *Festuca,* which has been cultivated for a long time and occurs in a range of colors and textures. Most of them form clumps of fine foliage, and the majority are strikingly bluish and quite hardy. They look good among rocks and as potted plants where their fine texture may be best admired.

I am very attracted to *Miscanthus sinensis* 'Zebrinus' (a grass of seven feet or so) because it has variegation in the form of horizontal bands, unusual in a monocot where striping is often parallel to the veining. This showy plant can look shaggy if it is not groomed. We chop ours to the ground yearly. There is also 'Variegatus' that exhibits parallel stripes of creamy yellow that run lengthwise on the leaf. This grass is an excellent tub subject, as containment lends a fountainlike form to the plant.

There is a rather rare non-grass bog plant called *Scirpus tabernaemontani zebrinus,* that has tubular stems of bright green, crossbanded in off-white. This plant flops over in a stiff breeze, but if I could grow only one bog plant in one perfect pot, it would be this! The stems are not jointed and quite fragile but the effect of the whole plant growing out of a mossy pot is unique and beautiful. It's an ideal terrarium subject.

From time to time somebody calls and says they have seen the most wonderful and gaily variegated bamboo ever, with white and pink stripes, growing wild somewhere and free for the digging. It always turns out to be *Arundo donax* 'Variegata', a plant I loathe from the disappointment of discovering that it is not a bamboo after all. However, it is a marvelous giant grass, and the new growth is rhubarb pink, fading into white margins on green leaves. It is a plant to be contained in a big tub, not only to give it form, but to keep it from invading the planet. Potbound, its coloring is perhaps more intense, and its form is that of a stately, erect fountain. In the ground it marches along resolutely, elbowing everything in sight. There is a solid green form which I dislike intensely.

If a person were so dedicated to variegation as to want an aggressive, variegated lawn, there is the following treat, the variegated St.

Augustine grass, *Stenotaphrum secundatum* 'Variegatum'. This grass, in its solid green form, is one of my least favorite plants. I understand one cannot play golf upon it as it is too lumpy. The variegated form grown as a pot plant with its extreme lemon yellow and bright green stripes, is a knockout. The idea of a lawn made out of this stuff is worse than a plaid blazer, striped shirt and paisley necktie, all worn simultaneously. That's how variegated it is and how assertive. It makes an excellent ground cover with larger potted plants, where you want just that proper touch of the vulgar.

There are a group of bamboos called *Sasa*. These are generally small, some less in height than a thick lawn, others easily maintained to under eight inches by a once-yearly shearing. The shearing also preserves the juvenile quality of this group of plants, thereby limiting the stem thickness to something like a toothpick, and also encouraging the growth of the new, beautifully marked, and colored foliage. These plants are unsurpassed as ground covers, wonderful as pot subjects, and perfect when used as bonsai companion plants as well as in dish gardens.

In a garden where walkways form an edge, these plants will not get away from you. In a less structured garden setting they should be restrained by subsoil barriers or grown in low containers. They count among their virtues an unsurpassed ability to hold the contours of steep terrain, and are able to prevent washouts of topsoil and the general unhinging of a three-dimensional landscape project.

Sasa (Sasaella) masasumiana albovariegata is one particular favorite. Its delicate stems are purplish, its foliage—which is slightly velvety—is strongly patterned in pale buttery stripes with a fine deep green pinstriping. In California, it is evergreen and plants are hardy to 0°F.

Years ago when I had but a single small clump I thought of it only as a pot plant, but now it grows outside the front door as an under planting for some giant timber bamboo, as well as in numerous tubs and pots. It is unusual to find such intense variegation

that is not at the same time gaudy or overwhelming.

Perhaps the next best plant of this type is *Arundinaria variegata* which has mostly ivory leaves pinstriped in deepest green. It is said to grow to four feet in height, something I have never observed. I grow this in the ground as well as in small pots and large tubs, just to make sure I am surrounded by it.

A. viridistriata is another bamboo of small stature whose new growth is both velvety in texture and is colored chartreuse, striped with green. After a summer the foliage ripens into almost solid green, which is why a yearly shearing is such a good thing to do. This plant also grows outside the front door in pots.

All of these small ground cover bamboos give an unmistakable Japanese touch to a garden. If you could play golf on these plants, I am sure it would put the sod-forming grasses out of business.

I am certain that mowed lawns have their place in the realm of gardening, particularly in North America where gardens have inherited a formal British tradition. I like to see those tightly formed gardens with neatly shaped hedges and velvet lawns, but only from a great distance or in photographs, because I am too lazy to work at this sort of thing.

Which brings me round to the subject of *Dichondra micrantha*. This substitute for lawn grass is a member of the morning glory family—although you could have fooled me—and grows into a glorious green carpet that is as flat as a table and never needs mowing. Unfortunately it is only hardy in Zone 10. I believe one cannot walk upon it so one must use stepping stones in order to wander through it. It is the only lawn I truly like to look at, and, alas, it isn't even a grass.

It isn't possible to write about something as familiar and dear to gardeners as grasses without enraging someone by omitting a particular favorite. And I must admit that if most lawn grasses were never mowed but permitted to grow to their full height as in a meadow, I would have nothing against them. It's just the mowing that I hate! ✒

A GREAT SCALE
FOR GRASSES

We tend to think of gardens and the plants they contain in terms more private than public. Wolfgang Oehme and James van Sweden have other ideas. The following article presents their views on ornamental grasses and designing gardens on a public scale. But their ideas work just as well in that small garden.

—P.L.

Wolfgang Oehme and James van Sweden

All of us spend as much time living in the community as we do in our homes. Yet we are surrounded in our cities by foolproof evergreen landscapes that are, as Christopher Lloyd says: ". . . a kind of living death." Such gardens could be revived with only one significant accommodation— by changing their viewpoint from a private to a public scale. Most of our firm's design concepts deal with space, whether for a layered effect, a four-seasons garden, or the sheer dynamism of plants. In fact, we believe that even intimacy belongs in the city and put plant combinations together on the biggest of sites just as we do on the smallest. By looking at the Federal Reserve garden in Washington, D.C., for example, people could learn about design for their own gardens.

What would you be looking for if you walked into one of our public gardens? First, you would check for balance. Are the evergreens and the deciduous plants in the correct proportion? In general, our garden designs are one-third evergreen. This

Wolfgang Oehme and James van Sweden are the owners of a Washington-based landscape-architect firm that has been the leading exponent of using ornamental grasses both in the home and in the commercial garden.

Pennisetum setaceum, fountain grass, is a lovely grass with attractive flowers and a graceful, arching form.   *Drawing by Peter Loewer*

approach is especially valuable in the winter when they are useful as backdrop to the dried ornamental grasses and their seed heads. They also define space, creating permanent layers of contrast for the changing layers of herbaceous plants, providing the deciduous effect that is so important on a large scale when summer lushness gives way to winter's elegant structures.

How interesting is the garden in every season? The public garden is on stage every day of the year and should always try to attract the passer-by. This is perhaps the most difficult aspect of design. Like choreographing a ballet, we try to visualize the design as moving across the palette of an entire year.

How are textures used to express the tactile character that is a central proposition of such gardens? In composition, the textures make a touchable structure of their own that ranges from the bold, upright sculpture of a yucca to the subtle flowers of the pendulous soft pennisetums to *Coreopsis* 'Moonbeam' with its finely cut leaves. Textural contrasts are even more important than color. We use it in bold, amorphous "cloud" masses to bring richness and focus to the design.

These three principles—balance, interest, and texture—are what make a garden. They help to create a personal scale that relates to nature. People go out to the garden to have lunch and relax, to meet someone and talk; they need a comfortable place to sit. We try to bring the scale of the city to a more personal level so that everyone will have a smaller space to anchor themselves, all amid the hustle and bustle about them. People can sit surrounded by plants and ornamental grasses and yet not feel hemmed in.

All of our designs are organized as a series of layered spaces that become progressively less architectural as they move out from a building. In public situations, we often plant trees well away from the building to create inner and outer areas. From more private spaces next to the building, the street view is softened; while from the street, screening layers create a scene worth exploring. Passers-by will discover interlocking volumes of planted and open spaces, boldly defined in a hurried city.

Boldness is the major difference to residential design, for the public garden must be "readable" at higher speeds and greater distances. Driving by, an undulating line of planting sweeps to the edge of the street, then dives deep into the garden, catching the eye like a fish on a hook. The garden should be dramatic when it's passed at 35 to 40 mph and it should also be beautiful from above. Our approach is to simplify the planting plan, using a smaller plant list in much bigger blocks of space for clarity and contrast.

On Pennsylvania Avenue we have relied, as usual, on a tough and disease-resistant planting list that doesn't call for a lot of maintenance. Such low maintenance must be a viable concept for gardens if we are to achieve a public landscape that is humane. Ornamental grasses grow in clumps that may need division about once in a decade but continue to maintain their scale without the help of pruning shears. With automated irrigation (every other night), and a feeding program, the ornamental grasses, perennials, shrubs and trees grow quickly and well. This is planned maintenance, an important part of a landscape architect's services.

Our firm has a long-term contract with the Pennsylvania Avenue Development Corporation to walk the avenue every week, noting problems and making suggestions. This is, of course, an ideal situation, but we always write a maintenance schedule for our projects—plant by plant and month by month—so that the maintenance staff can see exactly what they should do in every plant season. They won't cut down the beautiful winter garden in November; they'll feed each plant properly and allow it to develop naturally into its fullest form. It only takes one cycle for the staff to feel comfortable: it's a change in attitude and everyone stops hacking everything into shapes of balls and boxes. There are two big pluses to such plantings that impress maintenance people: ornamental grasses repel dogs and especially rats, whose burrows are invaded by the roots and people are less inclined to steal plants that look so natural in their settings.

Thirteen years ago, on the first public job for the firm, Jim asked Wolfgang what would happen when the rudbeckia grows into the pennisetum and tries to take over. Wolfgang answered: "They will fight it out!" And they did, calling it a draw. These plants develop at the same rate, both have vigorous root systems, and they tend to be so dense they crowd the weeds out, and they are also mulched well. Sometimes a black-eyed Susan peeks out from the pennisetums, making it all look like the blurred margins of a meadow.

Many urban sites aren't actually on the ground, but built over underground garages and on rooftops where the garden must be "built" over a sublevel structure. The Federal Reserve garden is such a place and demonstrates the wealth of plant life that's possible in light, shallow soil that is well fertilized, watered, and has good drainage.

Lately, we're more and more interested in combinations that explore how ornamental grasses, when used in large scale designs, become exclamation points or living sculptures separated from other masses of material on the ground plane. We have been inspired by Frank Stella in the design of a waterfront park in New York City, a jazzy score with great mounds of *Miscanthus strictus* used like staccato dots of gold. It's an effort to start a garden movement that reclaims the public landscape for the people—and we think it's about time. 🐟

Brooklyn Botanic Garden's monocot border contains (left to right) Miscanthus sinensis *'Gracillimus' and* Erianthus ravennae.

Ornamental grasses will not only survive, but thrive even in the hostile conditions of an upper story New York City terrace.

Not only are the ornamental grasses perfect for the typical suburban or country garden, they are also useful in city gardens where their linear forms and feathery flowers work perfectly against masses of metal and stone. The following is about grasses used in Rockefeller Center.　　　　—P.L.

Panicum virgatum, *switch grass, has an upright habit of growth that is light and airy and excellent autumn color.*

Grasses in the City

Linda Yang

The plantings seem natural enough—clumps of towering grasses which wave and rustle in the breeze. Yet this is no marshy seaside setting. Instead, these slender stems in tones of blue, gold, red and green, are a featured display at the Channel Garden in Rockefeller Center, where the wind that bends them to the pavement sweeps in between the Fifth Avenue skyscrapers.

The grasses were scheduled to remain in place for a number of weeks "depending on how they hold up," said Carl Miller, vice president of Rockefeller Center's Management Corporation, which oversees the dozen different landscape designs installed there each year. "If the grasses break or bend too much, our winter evergreens will be brought in to take their place."

The idea for a show of ornamental grasses was suggested to Mr. Miller by Edwina von Gal, a New York City landscape designer who said she first became fascinated with the plants after seeing them in a nursery field. Particularly effective in her design for the Channel Garden, are the scattered groups of tall, wheat-toned *Miscanthus sinensis,* which includes such cultivars as 'November Sunset', 'Silver Feather', and 'Silver Arrow'.

The grasses—which attract a lot of small city birds—are particularly beautiful at night, said Ms. von Gal.

Linda Yang is the author of the Terrace Gardener's Handbook, *a contributing writer to* The New York Times Home Section, *a photographer, and an expert at city gardening.*

Reprinted with permission from The Home Section *of* The New York Times, *October 24, 1985.*

The miscanthus grasses (*Miscanthus* spp.) are surrounded with plants of contrasting colors including the purple-plumed pennisetums *(Pennisetum setaceum),* the blue-toned wild rye *(Elymus glaucus)* along with the low growing variegated ribbon grass *(Phalaris arundinacea picta),* with its cool green and white stripes. There are also blue fescues (*Festuca* spp.), the golden-hued variegated Japanese sedge (*Carex morrowii* 'Old Gold') and the crimson-leaved Japanese blood grass *(Imperata cylindrica rubra).* Then when the Center's lights touch them they give an impression of an early winter sunset.

All of the plants in the display are hardy when used in the New York City area of USDA Zone of 7a with the exception of the stands of pampas grass *(Cortaderia selloana).* "If you have sun," she said, "they are all wonderful for the garden and they also tolerate moist, poorly drained soils."

The containers in which the grasses have been planted vary in depth between 18 and 20 inches, according to David Murbach, Rockefeller Center's division manager for gardening. This is the minimum size that terrace gardeners should use. The plants were grown especially for this display by Kurt Bluemel at his nursery in Maryland. They were balled and burlaped at the nursery and delivered to the city by truck.

All the plants in the Channel Garden are watered with cooled steam condensed from the air conditioners of Rockefeller Center. As a result they have received a commendation from the Environmental Action Coalition for helping to keep the city green.

Of Grasses

The following excerpt is from *The Book of Grasses* by Mary Evans Francis, published by Doubleday, Page & Company in 1912. It is a lovely book that deals with the beauty of most of the common American grasses and many of the sedges and rushes found from Canada southward to Virginia, and from the Atlantic coast westward to the Mississippi River.   —P.L.

Mary Evans Francis

From spring until late autumn grasses bloom by every wayside, and in field and meadow to form the green carpet of the earth. Widely distributed throughout all countries, and abundant even in faraway prehistoric days, grasses remain the most important family of the vegetable kingdom, and—of all common plants the most common—the least commonly known. Yet from the moment when the first violet lifts its blossom to the sunlight until in autumn the witch-hazel's delicate flowers are seen above fast-falling leaves, there is never a day when grasses are not in bloom, and never a week in summer when a score of different species may not be gathered.

In richness and variety of coloring, above their undertone of green, the blossoms and wind-blown anthers of the grasses rival in beauty the flowers that the wayfaring man collects. The grace of swaying stem and drooping leaf, the delicacy of tiny flowers tinged in rose and purple, and the infinite variety shown in form and coloring are lost upon those who are intent on seeking flowers that the forests make rare. Grasses there are, stout and higher than one's head, and grasses so slender that their dying stems among wayside weeds are

Calamagrostis x acutifolia *'Stricta', feather reed grass, is effective in a perennial border— this one at Brookside Gardens.*

like threads of gold; grasses whose panicles of bloom are more than half a yard in length, and of a color which only a midsummer sun can burn into August fields; grasses so stiff that winter's snow leaves them unbroken, and grasses so tiny that their highest flower is raised but a few inches from the soil.

Nearly one thousand species are found in the United States, nor is the study of these plants so difficult as it is thought to be. When accuracy in determining the individual species is desired, a small microscope and a few needles for dissecting the blossoms are all that is necessary. Even without these aids an intimate acquaintance with the grasses may be gained by observing only their most obvious characteristics of growth, and the various forms of flowering heads. Notice closely the grasses in a low meadow of early summer: the dense growth of green, hastily characterized as "grass," may contain many different species of this vast family, species which at a second glance are seen to have each their own distinguishing features.

Like charity the study of grasses may begin at home, and, like charity also, this most fascinating of nature studies may be carried far afield, for the grasses, most numerous of all flowering plants, we have always with us. Treelike in the tropics the bamboos, largest of the grass family, lift their blossoms 100 feet and more toward the sky; in cold countries mosslike grasses cringe and cling to the frozen ground, and through the temperate regions of the globe grasses grow in luxuriance of form and coloring and supply a background of green against which the world of trees and rivers, of brooks and ledges, is placed on colors ever changing, and ever perfect. Nature is continually busy reclaiming the unsightly places abandoned by man, covering with a garment of green the hillsides torn by rain, and carpeting with her "matted miracles of grass" the humble waysides.

The traditional spirit of the seasons is symbolized by outdoor coloring: cool, pale tints of early spring, rose color of June, warm tones of August fields, and a glory of purple and gold when the summer is past and the harvest ending. In all this continuity of change, which keeps the fact of Nature so new in its world-old familiarity, the grasses bear their part, and

Eragrostis spectabilis, *purple love grass, grows naturally in dry fields. It has a very large inflorescence for such a diminutive plant.*

as the violet and wild geranium of spring give place to midsummer hardhack, which in turn is pushed aside by goldenrod and asters, so the passing months bring fresh grasses into bloom and mark the calendar of the year by the flowering of these common plants.

It still is true, however, that:

"The world misprizes the too-freely offered And rates the earth and sky but carelessly."

Drawing by Peter Loewer

The dandelion is less honored than the arbutus, yet even the dandelion receives greater honor than do the early grasses, which aid in changing earth's wintry shroud to living green. Grasses yield us the earliest intimations of spring, as a faint flush of green, in harmony with the soft colors of April woods, tinges the brown hillsides before snows have ceased. The first grasses are more delicately colored than are those of midsummer when the sun burns red and purple into the tiny flowers. The green spikelets of many spring grasses depend for color upon their lightly poised anthers of lavender and gold. Sweet vernal grass, orchard grass, and june grass, so characteristic of spring, are succeeded by spreading panicles of hair grass, bayonetlike spikes of timothy and the richly colored red top whose blossoms burn with midsummer's warmth. September has still new grasses to offer, and in this month the beard grasses are conspicuous, as their stiff stems at last attain a growth that will enable them to withstand snow and frost. In many localities from 50 to 100 different grasses may be gathered, and, although, unlike the lilies, they do not flaunt their colors garishly, yet in rose and lavender, in purple and an infinite scale of green they rest and charm the eye with their beauty from April to October, when frosts bring to them new hues of brown and yellow in which they clothe the earth until green blades again push through spring turf.

Our waysides are the accepted gardens of many plants which, having followed the path of mankind through the New World, take the highways of civilization for their own, and find abundant means for transportation as seed is fastened on passers-by, or carried by the wind along smooth pathways. Few are the grasses that cannot be found in these wayside gardens as the roads wind through fertile country, from uplands to rich meadows, or pass sandy shores, where in a variety of soils the different grasses bloom and add a mass of verdure to the border of the way. Throughout the season these common gardens of the wayside hold a constantly changing procession of grasses; a procession which begins with low spear grass and

sweet vernal grass in April, and ends in October with the dropseed grasses and the beard grasses, although even in winter the species that remain standing may still be recognized.

Rarer flowers must be sought in deep woods and in hidden places in the swamps, but the cosmopolitan grasses are fitted to take up the struggle for existence wherever the seed chances to fall. Dean Herbert rightly says that "plants do not grow where they like best but where other plants will let them." By waysides we may see this struggle in its intensity as a dozen species strive for the same plot of ground and grow in tangles that include low cinquefoil and tall briars. The strife is always most intense between individuals of the same species, and here the grasses grow in profusion, occupying each inch of space, pushing out into deserted country roads, and spreading far and wide by means as interesting as ever the more noted flowering plants employ.

Bur-grass, with its thorny seed-burs, catches on passing objects and thus secures free portage to new fields; terrell-grass by thick, corky scales floats its seed upon the streams near which it grows; beach grass defines the sand to bury it and is found at the tops of the highest sand dunes, with whose rise it has kept pace, the long roots of the grass penetrating to the base of the dune; and couch-grass, sending sharp-pointed rootstocks rapidly through the soil, is a veritable "land-grabber."

Where the purslane and poppy produce a multitude of seeds from every flower, each blossom of the grass ripens but one, yet so richly stored is this with nutriment, and frequently so well protected against germination under unfavorable conditions, that the one seed may be worth many of those less perfectly equipped, since, in the process of evolution, diminution in the number of seeds is accompanied by an increase in the effectiveness of those that remain.

The twisted awns of certain grasses—e. g., sweet vernal grass and wild oats—show one of the most interesting mechanisms seen in the vegetable world. These awns, or bristlelike appendages of the grass flower, are extremely sensitive to atmospheric changes, and by their peculiar structure aid in burying the seed beneath the surface of the soil. In sweet vernal grass the scale, to which the ripened seed adheres, bears a brown awn, bent and twisted near its middle, and beset with minute, upward-pointing hairs on its basal part. Such awns are strongly hygroscopic and during cold or dry weather remain tightly twisted, thus holding the seed where it chances to be. Under the influence of moisture the awn untwists and by its rotation drives the fallen seed slowly but surely beneath the soil. Although dry weather may follow, causing the awn to became twisted again, the upward-pointing hairs catch on particles of earth or grass and, holding the seed down, prevent it from being drawn up. Thus it lies ready for the next shower when the awn pushes the seed farther into the earth. This peculiarity of structure is easily observed without the aid of the microscope. If a few of the ripened seeds are laid upon the moistened palm of the hand they will immediately begin to move, as if alive, and the rotating of the awn can be plainly seen. Interesting experiments have been made whereby it has been seen that in sand, alternately wet and dried, the awns of certain grasses will bury the seed several inches beneath the surface.

Each locality shows characteristic grasses, and as in a short walk we pass from low meadows to dry hillsides we find new species to excite fresh interest. On sea beaches we look for the long, gray-green leaves of marram grass, or beach grass, for spreading clumps of sea-beach panic grass, for the dark, wiry stems of fox grass, and for rigid-leaved grasses of hot sands. Salt marshes show dense jungles of reedlike grasses, creek sedge, salt reed grass, and the tall reed. Dry hillsides are covered in spring by wild oat grass and wavy hair grass, where later purple finger grass sheathed rush grass, and stiff beard grasses will bloom. In dry fields we look for the low growth of the smaller panic grasses, for the slender, one-sided spikes of field paspalum, and for wide-spreading panicles of purple eragrostis. Borders of woodlands offer poverty grass, black oat grass, and muhlenbergias, while in deep woods we search for shade-loving grasses,

the tall, slender bottlebrush grass, the lower mountain rice, and the nodding fescue. Marshy meadows are full of interest to the student of grasses: reed canary grass with broad, blue-green leaves borders narrow brooks, and nearby the blue-joint grass, slender and stiff, rises bearing narrow, deeply colored panicles; graceful manna grasses fill the marshes of early summer, and later the rough leaves and stems of rice cut grass form tangled masses in low grounds. By river borders grows the great grama grass whose leaves are so broad as to resemble those of our cultivated corn, and in wet soil, also, is found the tall Indian rice on which the reed-bird feeds. A country dooryard of an acre may show more than a dozen different grasses, while in the garden near half a score of other species invade the cultivated land and weeds. A large collection of grasses, preserved either as herbarium specimens or in the more artistic impression made upon photographic paper, may be gathered in a short time, and differences perhaps little noticed by the casual observer will seem marked indeed to the student who at the close of a summer's study will deem it as unpardonable to mistake one of our commom grasses for another as to mistake an elm for an oak.

Corn, wheat, oats, the day of the first cultivation of these cereal grains long antedates history, and how seldom is it realized that they are grasses. Virgil and Columella wrote long ago of the care of meadows and fields. Indeed the word cereal stands as an article of faith in the goddess Ceres, who searched with torches for the grain carried off by winter frost, and on finding the seed raised it to its flower once more. Bertha was the Ceres of German mythology, and winds and rains affecting crops were believed to be under her control. Corn spirits there were which were symbolized under the forms of wolves and goat-legged creatures, similar to classic satyrs. To the older peasantry of Germany and Russia these corn spirits still haunt and protect the fields which show the "Grass wolf" or "Corn wolf" to be abroad when the wind, as it passes, bends the grass and the ripening grain. The last sheaf of rye is occasionally left afield as shelter for the "Roggenwolf," or "Rye wolf," and it is not long since the Iceland farmer guarded the grass around his fields lest the mischievous elves, hiding among the grasses, and ever waiting to harm him, should invade his cultivated land.

In old herbals the word *grass, gres, gyrs* meant any green plant of small size, and though we have restricted the meaning of the word it still is carelessly applied to a multitude of sedges and rushes which in manner of growth and form of flower differ markedly from the true grasses. To the casual observer the grasses are but "grass," and to few is their diversity, their beauty, and their value apparent. We are blind to the infinite variety shown by nature in these common plants, of which we often know scarcely more than do the cattle that feed upon them; yet on no other family of flowering plants does the beauty of the green earth and its adaptation as a home for man so largely depend. ❧

Pennisetum alopecuroides, *perennial fountain grass, is planted along the fence in Longwood Gardens' Idea Garden.*

Ornamental Grasses in the Rock Garden

Louis Budd Myers

The following articles both deal with grasses for the rock garden. Mr. Myers points out that even the rock garden purist has something to learn from growing grasses, and Dr. Nixon hastens to add more grasses to that fire. It is interesting to note that together they speak of 27 different grasses and only overlap on two choices, *Eleocharis parbula* and *Hakonechloa macra* 'Aureola', both of those grasses being particularly beautiful. —P.L.

At a recent rock garden lecture, the speaker, with a tone that suggested a raised eyebrow, stated that he had heard of some people who are growing *grasses* in their rock gardens. It is true that rock gardening has its purists and has come to mean, among other things, the attempt to grow the difficult flowering plants of alpine regions, but rock gardening can mean also having a good time and creating settings that please the eye. Some easier-to-grow plants are a blessing.

A friend, many years ago, told me that sempervivums are the binder that hold the rock garden together. He was referring to their many uses: to conceal cracks between rocks, to hold back edging soils, as well as to be decorative. I find that some grasses work in a similar way. Other grasses are beautiful enough to be used as accents. I have chosen 12 grasses that I enjoy above all others.

Louis Budd Myers is a well-known rock gardener. He was for thirty-three years an editor and writer on the staff of a national biographical encyclopedia and has contributed many articles to the American Rock Garden Society, The Conifer Society *and other scholarly journals.*

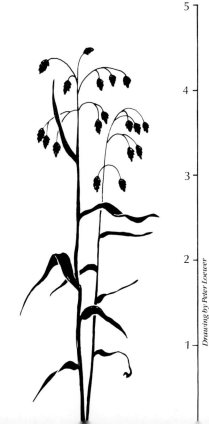

Drawing by Peter Loewer

Chasmanthium latifolium *(left), northern sea oats, is about two feet high with large flattened seed heads rising above the leaves. It is often cut for dried bouquets.*

Right: Hakonechloa macra *'Aureola' makes a striking accent wherever it is planted.*

Bouteloua gracilis (blue grama) a type of forage grass of the prairies, has several appealing features. Its flowering heads rise about 20 inches from a dense tuft of grayish green, fine leaves that twist about in a curly tangle. The heads grow at almost a right angle to the stem. They look like lacerated flags, each with a fringe of purplish stamens hanging in a row. After ripening each resembles a row of eyelashes. The stems dart here and there, winking in the wind. *Bouteloua* is distinctly graceful and enhances an open alpine lawn. Individual plants of lower stature can be found.

Carex comans is one of the two New Zealand natives to survive in my Poconos rock garden, the other being *Geranium sessiliflorum nigrum*. Both are brown-leafed plants. This carex also has a green form, but the brown form comes true from seed. This form always fosters the illusion of fall or winter for most onlookers. Its foliage is tannish brown deepening to rusty-orange tones toward the base. Its innumerable leaf blades fountain out from the base and are more than a foot long. It is a mistake to cut back the foliage at any time since the plant is evergreen (ever brown?) and the cut basal stems never wholly disappear. The plant is decorative anywhere that one wants a soft accent. It looks particularly good against gray stone. Its flowering stems are strangely attenuated, each much longer than the leaf blades. A stem appears to reach out and almost plant its seed heads in the soil. I have found few seedlings.

Carex plantaginea, a native plant, prefers moisture and some shade. It is one of the first plants that was introduced into my childhood rock garden. I found it fascinating and unique because of the rippling or puckering of the leaf between leaf veins, an effect that resembles seersucker. It can form a carpet if the soil is rich and loamy, but it can be kept to a single plant with diligence. The leaf blades can reach some 10 inches in length. Its inflorescence is insignificant, although brightly spiky with yellowed stamens.

Chasmanthium latifolium, (Uniola

Drawing by Peter Loewer

70

Chasmanthium latifolium

latifolia) a common and longtime favorite of American gardeners, is called northern sea oats or wild oats. About two feet tall, it has grasslike basal blades which are slightly glaucous. Its large, flattened oatlike seed heads, suspended on thin arching stems, flutter and twist in the slightest breeze. The movement is so refreshing that the plant should be in every garden. It will take a lot of shade and likes a woodland setting. It is best known for its use in dried winter bouquets.

Dactylis glomerata variegata, which is striped white and a pale green, would appear to come in various forms. The one that I grow stays diminutive. It was planted on the edge of a nest of sempervivums on the lower reaches of a scree bed. As both plants have multiplied, the *Dactylis* has come to pop up in low tufts here and there among the "semps." Recently *Ephedra minuta,* a small gymnosperm, has begun to invade the bed, and the result is delightful. *Dactylis* is easily removed from scree. I would be very careful about planting it in any other type of soil mix unless measures were taken to keep in confined.

Eleocharis parvula is tiny and easily overlooked. It grows on the moist verge of the small rock garden bog. After many years it has formed a clump some three inches across. A sedge, it is a very close relative of the Chinese water chestnut. Each hairlike spikelet is about an inch long. Its name is derived from the Greek words meaning marsh and grace. It is widely distributed. A wallower in bog heaven, it comes from the edges of muddy ponds.

Hakonechloa macra 'Aureola', a native of Japan is an outrageous beauty. Although Hakonechloa is a difficult name to master, in Japan it is known as Urahagusa Zoku. It grows on wet rock cliffs in mountains but is amenable to a variety of garden conditions. Its overall beauty: coloration, form, and mobility in a breeze, is paramount. *H. m.* 'Aureola' is striped with a vibrant yellow and a pleasant green and each leaf-blade edge becomes suffused with rosy pink. Rainbow or peacock grass would make apt common names. It mul-

71

tiplies quite rapidly by stolons but is not rampant. A small beginning clump may become a foot or more across at the base in a few years; the arching leaf blades make the clump appear to be almost twice that size across. Each six- to-eight-inch leaf blade comes from a stem that has slightly thickened nodes at the axil and resembles bamboo. This grass should be planted in a special place, perhaps against a background of dwarf evergreens, somewhere in a niche of its own.

Juncus mertensianus also graces the rock garden bog and must be watched diligently or potted in a container which has been sunk in the bog. If one has a large bog or a poolside for planting, it need not be restrained so forcibly. Although it has the usual rushlike leaf spikes, its seed head is elegant—quite large and purplish black, not unlike a flattened, shiny, black raspberry. It is 10 inches or less in height.

Luzula spicata, an alpine or subalpine rush, does not look like a rush. It forms a caespitose heap of slightly falcate, or curved hairy basal leaves. The hairs of this attractive plant lend a silvery sheen. *Luzula* can be used wherever the soil is slightly dry, acid and the site is shady.

Panicum clandestinum, the corn or deer's-tongue grass, forms large, dense clumps. Like many panic grasses, its broad leaves taper to a point and project at intervals up the stem. It must be placed carefully in the rock garden, because of its height which can reach three feet. I cut back my plant in midsummer—the subsequent growth is shorter and more dense. The late fall coloring of this grass, at least in my garden, is magnificent—leaves smeared a deep, vibrant claret with tan and green patches. The color persists long after the leaves are cut for bouquets.

Stenophyllus capillaris, a true annual and the only member of this genus, is a spiky hedgehog of rigid looking hairlike stems. The plants vary in size, from minute to eight inches in height and width, depending on the soil. Those that seed in a trough in my garden stay tiny. The grass can seed anywhere but is so easily removed that it poses no threat.

Stipa tenuifolia, an annual in my garden, is exceptionally beautiful. Another fountaining type, this grass has numerous hairlike,

Carex comans *provides a decorative accent wherever a soft accent is needed.*

one-foot-long leaf blades on each plant. Aside from its soft, airy quality, *Stipa tenuifolia* is a pleasing light green color, an apple green, quite unlike anything else in the garden. Everyone is attracted by it.

With the passing of years certain grass clumps expand beyond the accepted confines. I recently established a rock garden of grasses, a bed dominated by a large rock. In this new garden I have planted the garden overflow and have added certain other taller and more invasive grasses that are not suited to the older garden. The grasses, brought together in this way, in all sizes and colorations, are a new delight. Examples remain in the established rock garden as small specimens.

Some Grasses for the Rock Garden

Dr. C. William Nixon

There are literally hundreds of grasses that have potential as rock garden subjects. Fortunately, there are criteria that, if applied, limit the scope.

The criteria I have used to narrow the field comprise the following:

Size of Grass: The grass *must* be of a size that is small enough to fit into most rock gardens or smaller still for a trough planting.

Uniqueness: The grass should be different in some way.

Form: Size and uniqueness along with the shape or growth habit combine to give the plant's "form" which is important in judging the suitability of a grass as a rock garden subject.

Habit of Increase: Grasses can be invasive from both seed dispersal and stolons. Stolons are usually underground and often go undetected until it is too late. On the other hand, there are grasses that utilize these same methods of increase but not to such excess that they become pests. And then there are a few grasses that are so difficult to grow that this can become a negative factor.

Color: In addition to the shades of green, grasses come in other colors and combinations. There are those with red, yellow, gold or white, often in various combinations with green or, sometimes, entirely of a color other than green. These colors are important in the positioning or placement of a grass. For instance, white (or even gold or yellow) will show up best with a dark background and, happily, a dark corner may be significantly brightened by these same grasses. Also,

---

Dr. C. William Nixon is the founder, editor and publisher of the Sempervivum Fanciers Association Newsletter, *the author of a number of scientific articles, a research consultant in animal genetics and a general all-around plantsman.*

Festuca ovina glauca, *blue fescue, is the bluest of all grasses and one of the finest for rock gardens. There are many named cultivars from which to select.*

included here are the hirsute and woolly grasses as these characteristics can impart a gray color to what would otherwise be a green plant.

Personal Preference: A subjective criterion but an important one.

The Grasses

Alopecurus lanatus (woolly foxtail grass) is very difficult to grow. It is mentioned because it is a densely woolly (and therefore gray in color) grass. Originating in the mountains of Spain, it is probably not winter hardy throughout much of the United States and should be grown in a trough that can be moved to an alpine house or cold frame in winter. By doing this, it will also keep the winter wet off the woolly leaves and crown, another requirement for this touchy plant. Grow it in extremely gritty soil with a generous amount of chippings around the crown. It grows only to about four inches high and is a very slow grower.

Arrhenatherum elatius bulbosum 'Variegatum' (bulbous oat grass) is a very attractive and striking grass, but the *only* form of the species worth growing. Usually attaining a height of about a foot, this plant has narrow white-striped leaves. It is easy to grow, and, if it has any fault, it is that it can spread rather rapidly by means of bulbils that form at the base. These fall off and root. Grow in full sun and a lean soil mixture to keep it in bounds. Hardy to Zone 5 at least.

Deschampsia flexuosa 'Aura' (yellow wavy hair grass). This is the yellow form of wavy hair grass and is far more attractive than the normal green plant. The yellow form was discovered a few years ago in the mountains of Czechoslovakia and named 'Aura'. You will likely find it called 'Aurea'. My plants have never grown over a foot in height. They form dense clumps of very fine leaves that remain during the winter. It prefers acid soil and seems to be happy in sun or shade. This form, 'Aura,' comes true from seed, and it may also be propagated by division of the clump. Hardiness should be no problem.

Eleocharis parvula (spike rush) is a dwarf sedge. It grows to one inch in height and prefers wet feet (It will even grow under water!). This tiny plant is obviously a good subject for a wet trough or a boggy area. It is attractive and quickly forms lovely green mats when in a desirable location. It may invade moist areas and should be watched carefully. Hardy to Zone 5.

Equisetum scirpoides and *E. scirpoides* 'Curly' (dwarf horsetail), the smallest species of *Equisetum,* grow only four to six inches high. Plants of this species must be kept constantly moist, and like most horsetails, can be invasive when in the right conditions. *E. scirpoides* is a tiny and attractive plant whose hollow stems stand straight up. However, the 'Curly' form is even nicer as the stems are contorted and wavy, tending to go in all directions. Consequently, 'Curly' is not quite as tall as the type plant. Hardy to Zone 5.

Festuca ovina var. *glauca* (blue fescue) is one of the best grasses for the rock garden. It is the bluest of all grasses and one of the finest. There are many named cultivars of slightly different sizes and degrees of blueness—all worth growing. This is a perennial evergreen grass usually attaining somewhere between 6 and 12 inches in height, and hardy to Zone 4. It requires full sun and perfect drainage. Give it a gravelly sandy soil. The leaves are blue, slender, stiff, and spiky. The plant grows naturally as a tight clump that slowly increases its size and is non-invasive. Increase it by dividing the clump. Although self-sown seedlings are often found, they may vary considerably from the parent in size and degree of blueness. However, they are almost always attractive and garden worthy. Unfortunately, plants sold under this name are often something else.

Hakonechloa macra 'Aureola' is one of the most strikingly colorful grasses. The leaves are flat, narrow and graceful, and tend to arch in the same direction giving the impression that the wind is blowing. This is an added attraction, and careful attention is advised when situating it. The precise leaf color is almost indescribable. Each leaf is irregularly streaked lengthwise with green and cream-yellow. In good light, much of the leaf turns pink or even bronze. However, this grass prefers some shade. Grow it in a rich, well-drained compost with no lime. It reaches a height of 12 to 24 inches. Propagate by dividing the clump since it spreads slowly and non-invasively by underground stolons. This is a lovely plant and is hardy to Zone 4.

Holcus mollis 'Albovariegatus' (white variegated velvet grass) is the best small variegated grass, a deciduous perennial, growing only to about four inches. A broad pure white stripe runs on both edges of the leaf with a narrow green stripe running down the center. When happy, it produces many long underground rhizomes and can spread rather quickly, but it is worth the problems it might cause. The typical non-variegated plant, *H. mollis,* is a terribly invasive weed and has no garden merit. Fortunately, 'Albovariegatus' is more restrained and far more attractive. Hardy to Zone 5.

Imperata cylindrica 'Rubra' (Japanese bloodgrass) is a lovely medium-size grass. It was not supposed to be winter hardy so in the early years it was wintered in a cold frame or indoors. As it became more abundant, many of us began leaving clumps outdoors in winter and, although it was completely deciduous, it reappeared in spring. From personal experience, I know that is has survived in Zone 5 to 6. The clump increases rather slowly. The leaf blades are green at the base but turn blood red at the ends of all the leaves. This grass is most spectacular if placed where the evening sun is behind it, causing the red leaves to glow. Propagate by dividing the clump.

Lagurus ovatus 'Nanus' (dwarf hare's tail grass). The 'Nanus' form, an annual, is a miniature version six inches or less of the larger *L. ovatus* which may reach two feet. Plant the seed in spring where the plant is to grow, and it will produce its lovely inflorescences in late summer. The foliage is unremarkable but its many flower or seed heads look like little rabbits' tails. It makes the best show if grown in bunches or patches. It is a choice small grass, but the seed may be difficult to locate.

Mibora minima (early sand grass) is a tiny annual grass that grows to a four-inch maximum and usually less. If happy, it produces seeds quite heavily. The tiny plants appear early in the growing season and quickly reach maturity. By early summer, it is in flower, seeds promptly, and then usually dies. Where it is moist, it may remain green for a longer time. Although this plant seeds itself, it has a shallow root system making it easy to pull out. It makes neat little tuffets, with tiny, hairlike leaves that are wiry. This is also a useful plant for troughs where the little clumps impart a natural turf appearance. It seems to prefer to grow in rocky or gravelly soil.

Milium effusum aureum (Bowles' golden grass) is an extremely showy grass and easy to grow. It attains a height of about a foot and has rather broad leaves that are a glowing golden yellow. The intensity of color varies during the season but is most vivid in spring. Depending on the severity of the winter, the leaves may not die back. Trim back in early spring before growth begins, since the new leaves are the most brilliant. It is hardy to at least Zone 5 to 6. This plant comes true from seed, and, if one does not want it seeding around liberally, the stalks should be cut off before seed ripens. It may also be propagated by dividing the clump. The showy nature of this grass is enhanced by the setting sun.

Poa abbreviata is the smallest of any of the true grasses listed above. Its specific name is descriptive as it grows only one to two inches high. It is perennial and survives in Zone 5 to 6. Propagate by dividing the clump or from seed which it occasionally sets. This little charmer makes a dense mat or turf similar to some of the larger lawn grasses. It then spreads laterally by underground runners. Its dark green leaves are tiny spikes that are more soft than rigid. Because of its similarity to lawn-type grasses, it can be used in the smaller rock garden or trough to create the effect of an alpine lawn.

Zoysia tenuifolia (Korean grass) is a small *Zoysia* that is much more fine and delicate than its coarse and more familiar relative, *Zoysia japonica*. *Z. tenuifolia* forms a thick, dense carpet of emerald green. According to references, it is not at all winter hardy. I found it growing as a tough and beautiful lawn grass in southern California. My plants have survived a winter here in Massachusetts (Zone 5 to 6) in a coldframe. Ultimately, I will try it outdoors, but not until it becomes better known and tried in many areas. It is probably hardy in the milder sections of the country and need not be limited to the deep south. It increases by rather long above-ground runners that root down at each node.

Final Comments

In the foregoing list of grasses I have not included any of the bamboos. Most are either too large for the average rock garden or else too invasive. Some are both. Many are not reliably winter hardy in colder areas. *Arundinaria viridistriata* was the only bamboo considered and this one only in one of its dwarf and more brilliantly colored forms. It is bright yellow and lights up the whole area especially when the light is dim such as evening or early morning. It appears to be winter hardy in my area (Zone 5 to 6), but it can be terribly invasive and should be watched closely. Due to its apparent variation in height and brilliance of coloring, search for the most desirable form or clone. They do vary, and it is a good idea to see this one growing before purchasing.

There are many grasses that have not been mentioned. Large and medium-to-large grasses have been omitted. Most are specimen plants and, except for unusual spots in larger rock gardens, are more attractive for the perennial border. There are a few genera of medium-to-small grasses that one might wish to investigate: *Acorus, Carex, Festuca* (fescues), *Juncus, Luzula* (wood rushes), *Melica* (melics) and *Poa*. Any reference books on grasses will suggest many others.

Grasses of
Yesteryear

The following articles are taken from *The Ladies Floral Cabinet* published in New York City. This was an 11- by 14- inch newsletter of 24 pages, published monthly and dealing with houseplants and garden plants plus a new piece of sheet music bound into every issue. —P.L.

A nineteenth century couple admires some pampas grass.

A grass garden in a cup and saucer.

January, 1880:
New and Rare Plants

Of the many new and beautiful plants introduced to this country within the last few years, the *Eulalia japonica zebrina*,* figured in this number, is certainly the most ornamental. It is exceedingly rare to find a plant with so many recommendations for popular favor. The plant is a hardy herbaceous perennial, of rapid growth, and of the most graceful habit. It grows from four to six feet in height. The flower stalks appear in September, with terminal panicles of brownish flowers, gracefully curved to one side, not unlike the ostrich plume. When dry, these flowers will last for years, making them particularly desirable for winter bouquets. A singular feature of this plant, as will be seen by the engraving, is the variegation, which is unlike that of any other plant, being across the leaf, instead of running longitudinally or of being in irregular blotches; these markings are regular and distinct, of creamy white with deep green, producing a most singular and pleasing effect. Without any exceptions, it is the most desirable and appropriate plant for the lawn yet introduced. This plant was discovered and brought out from Japan by Thomas Hogg, Esq., whose extensive researches there has given us many of our most popular plants, among the number being the hydrangea that bears his name, also the new climbing hydrangea. We are under obligations to Peter Henderson & Co., who first sent this plant out, for the illustration.

July, 1882:
Juncus zebrinus†, or Porcupine Plant

This remarkable plant is a native of Japan, and was first introduced to cultivation by Thomas

* *Eulalia japonica zebrina* now *Miscanthus japonicus* 'Zebrinus'

† *Juncus zebrinus* now *Juncus effusus* 'Zebrinus'

Hogg, Esq., of New York, who brought it with him some years since on his return from that country. He sent the whole stock to England, where "novelties" of merit are more highly appreciated than in this country, thus awarding the collector more liberally. This plant has a most peculiar appearance when growing, the idea suggested by a group of it being that of a cluster of porcupine quills, whence its common name. The plant, which is a true rush, throws up erect, terete leaves, but these instead of being green, are transversely banded with white and green, the colors being in most cases pretty evenly distributed; sometimes the white predominates, the surface being either wholly white, or the green bands being narrower and less conspicuous, but in the best marked leaves the green and white portions occupy alternately nearly equal bands of about half an inch deep. It is a most interesting plant, and being so entirely distinct and effective, it will, without doubt, come into general use, not only as an ornamental plant for the garden, but as a pot plant, and for window gardens, in hanging baskets, vases or other designs for growing plants.

For an opportunity to illustrate this plant we are under obligations to Messrs. Hallock, Son & Thorpe, of Queens, N.Y., who have imported recently from its native habitat a large quantity, which they intend soon to offer to the trade and all others in search of this rare and beautiful plant. Messrs. Hallock & Thorpe consider this plant perfectly hardy. If so, it will greatly enhance its value.

From Vick's Illustrated Magazine *of the late 1800s comes the following letter about another popular grass of the last century, pampas grass.* —P.L.

Dear Mr. Vick:

I had no idea of the beauty of pampas grass until I came South to live. I now have in my garden the plumes that stand, I am quite sure, ten feet from the ground, while the leaves make a mound-like mass, certainly six feet in height. I don't know, but I presume that this grass is more natural to warm countries. I have a plant, or, perhaps a mass of plants, that now have forty of its beautiful spikes. These spikes, however, are not as beautiful as those I have seen in in the North, for they are not silvery-white, but a dull, greenish color, and do not look well when gathered for winter. What makes the difference? I do not know.

Mrs. S. E. I., Texas

Answer: Pampas grass‡, *Gynerium argenteum,* is a native of South America. The common name is given because it grows abundantly on the vast plains of that country, called Pampas. It was brought to this country and Europe about thirty years ago, and is now prized and cultivated wherever it can be grown successfully. It will not bear severe northern winters, and perhaps, cannot be grown successfully north of Philadelphia. The best plumes, such as are sold by florists for winter ornaments, and which are really beautiful, are grown in California, and their silvery-whiteness is obtained by bleaching. A few days' exposure to the sun removes all color. In this way all the grasses can be bleached, while those that it is thought best to keep in the natural color must be dried in the shade. The everlastings, also, should be cured in the shade.

‡ *Gynerium argenteum,* now *Cortaderia selloana*

In 1884, the Ladies' Floral Cabinet Co. of New York, published a book entitled: Window Gardening. *The following material on Home Ornaments is taken from the fourteenth edition.* —P.L.

This department would not be complete without a word for the little ones of the house, some hint to them of what they can do to bring forth some glowing spot or sprig of living greenery. So we tell them how to make some pretty little contrivances in grasses, etc.

Plants with light, graceful foliage are every year becoming more popular; and to complete a picture of the highest order one requires a great variety of colors, and graceful pencilings; so in window gardening the culture of grasses adds greatly to the whole effect. Their feathery plumes may not possess brilliancy of coloring, but their silvery and emerald tints are an offset to their more gorgeous companions.

Far prettier than many a pretentious and costly ornament is a simple bowl of grasses planted in pine cones, set in sand, in moss or common soil.

If grown in cones—procure them from the woods, and sprinkle in as much soil as their scales will retain; then scatter the grass seeds over it, and sprinkle with water; place the cones in sand or moss—and be sure that they do not become dry—but water them sparingly at first, once a day, and set in a moderately warm place. Soon the seeds will sprout, and the tiny spears protrude in every direction.

Grass will sprout and grow in pine cones without any soil, but it serves to prevent the cone from closing too tightly when sprinkled, and also makes a more vigorous growth. The cones can be suspended in a window, either singly or in groups of three fastened together with thread or wire; or a rustic basket or stand can be procured, and filled with cones with different kinds of grass, growing in each cone. There are three thousand different species of grasses in the world, and their study is a pleasing pursuit.

A very charming effect can be produced by placing a wet sponge in a glass bowl, and sprinkling over it canary seed, grass and flax seeds;

Zebra grass from a nineteenth century illustration.

Miscanthus sinensis *'Zebrinus'*

A more formal grass garden with seeds planted in pine cones.

soon it will be covered with a thick growth of fresh bright green; it must be judiciously watered; if kept too dry it will wither away; if too wet it may damp off. Mustard seed may also be used, and its tiny yellow blossoms, will be to many, a novelty as well as a delight.

Children and invalids can derive much pleasure from raising a grass garden; it is better to select the dwarf varieties, as the taller kinds require more nourishment.

A tumbler garden may be constructed as follows: Fill a common tumbler or goblet with water, cut out a round of cotton batting, or of soft thick flannel of just the size to cover the surface, and lay it gently upon the water, upon this scatter the seeds of grass, or flax, or mustard, or all mixed, and gently set the tumbler away in a dark place. In a few days the seed will start; soon the roots will begin to penetrate the cotton or flannel, slowly sending down their delicate white fibers to the bottom of the vessel, while the top will be covered with a little thicket of green; after the second day the vessel must be kept in a warm tight place, and two or three times a week carefully replenished with water by means of a teaspoon, or syringe inserted beneath the edge of the flannel.

A great advantage of such a miniature garden as this is that the roots may be plainly seen growing through the cloth. Watercress has been grown this way, and a little story is related of a little girl who kept her invalid mother supplied all winter long with watercress grown in this way on wet flannel.

Porcupine grass from a nineteenth century illustration.

Annual Grasses for Garden and Bouquet

Few plants add more charm to a garden than the annual ornamental grasses. These are species grown not for the leaves but instead for the seemingly unending variety of their flowers.

Peter Loewer

Last night as I climbed the stairs in our old farmhouse I heard a rustle of dried leaves from atop the antique chest that sits in the corner by the banister. There our cat, Maude, was busily taking turns at pushing the cracked majolica vase towards the chest's edge and batting about the large bouquet of dried grasses that the vase contained.

Thwack! And a foot-long stem with the heavy seedhead of some foxtail millet snapped in three pieces. Swish! And the lovely silvery-bronze panicles of goldentop shattered in a hundred shards. I sprang forward but before I could reach the action, the black sorghum seeds stuck in her claws and the whole affair shot up towards the ceiling. Then with the synchronization of a fine watch, Maude pirouetted on a point in mid-air at the same instant that the pot and grasses smashed on the floor.

A bouquet of dried seed heads of annual grasses will last all winter in the house. The individual grasses are discussed on page 86.

Drawing by Peter Loewer

I couldn't be angry about it. The vase was broken to begin with and the cat spinning in the air within a shower of grass seeds was both high drama and entertainment rolled into one. Besides it was already January and in a few months the snow would melt and the sun warm the garden where these ornamental grasses are sown every season.

Of all the flowers in our garden the favorites are the annual ornamental grasses. Unlike their perennial relatives, these plants are rarely grown for their foliage which, except for the ornamental corns, looks weedy at best, but instead for the endless variety of their flowers and seeds. Whether planted out to relieve our dependence on the typical bedding annuals or to be gathered and dried for winter bouquets, the annual grasses deserve a place in many more gardens.

As a general rule, plants need a position with full summer sun for adequate growth and flowering, but they are not too fussy about soil conditions. As long as the soil drains and is capable of supporting a good crop of weeds, the annual grasses do quite well.

I usually start most of the seeds indoors in early spring since our local growing season only guarantees 90 to 120 days between frosts. In warmer climates, the seeds can be planted directly into the ground in April and on into May.

When planting these annual grasses prepare and mark the seedbed with care. The new little plants look like any other grassy weed, which can lead to endless confusion and dismay. I was careless one year and lost almost a whole crop of hare's-tail grass to the strangling stolons of crabgrass before I realized what was afoot.

As seedlings grow to one and two inches tall, thin them to six or twelve inches between each plant, depending on the ultimate height. Wild oats, for example, should be about one foot apart, while the hare's-tail grass is happy in a six-inch space. Also, be generous with the seed—the smaller grasses look better when planted in substantial drifts of the same species. Remember to collect seed for coming seasons. Because none of these grasses are hybrids, all will grow true from seed. Store them in carefully marked packages (stamp or coin envelopes are excellent) in a cool, dry place.

The drawing illustrates the following grasses: (1) Foxtail millet *(Setaria italica)* grows between two and four feet tall and looks exactly like the foxtail that teenagers of the 1930s tied on the rumble seats of their old Ford coupes. The dense panicles are often up to a foot in length and bow towards the earth with the weight of the seeds. While the plants are tolerant to some dryness, they perish quickly under drought conditions. This particular grass was cultivated in Ancient China (2700 BC), reached Europe during the Middle Ages, and in 1849 entered the United States, where it has become an important fodder crop. The seed is harvested for bird feed. A group of these grasses is stunning in the garden border and a bowl full of the panicles can make a striking addition to a room lasting as long as you have the patience to dust them or until your cat decides to play.

(2) Variegated corn (*Zea mays* 'Variegata') grows up to six feet tall, but usually hovers between three or four. Unlike the other annual grasses, it is grown for its beautifully shaded leaves that are striped with green, red, pink, and wide bands of pure white. The cobs never grow very large; the silk just adds interest to the plants. Corn is a heavy feeder,

so unlike the other grasses, fertile soil is needed and never skimp on the water. Try growing these corns in eight-inch pots, grouping them on the terrace for an effective outdoor decoration.

(3) Goldentop *(Lamarckia aurea)* will grow about 20 inches tall. Named after J.B. Lamarck, the naturalist who lost out to Darwin in the evolutionary sweepstakes, goldentop is my favorite flower both for cutting and the front of the border. The one-sided panicles have a shimmering look when fresh and become a tarnished silver-green with age. By midsummer the plants are turning brown, so a second crop should be prepared. The flowers shatter easily when dry so be sure to pick them before they mature. Goldentop is found growing as a weed in the southwestern United States.

(4) Quaking grass *(Briza maxima)* reaches three feet in height during a good summer season. A native of southern Europe, this grass has been in cultivation as a garden ornament for well over 200 years. The spikelets shake and quiver with every gentle motion of the breeze. They are faintly striped with purple and a most attractive addition to the bouquet. Quaking grass should be limited to the cutting garden—it's a bit too ungainly for a prominent place in the garden proper. Pick the panicles before they open.

(5) Brome grass *(Bromus madritensis)* will reach two feet in height. It is one of a number of species in the genus eminently qualified for both garden and vase. The flowers retain all their grace when dried, and the leaf tips of the species shown become tinged with auburn as they ripen. There are usually three or four species listed in seed catalogs.

(6) Hare's-tail grass *(Lagurus ovatus)* grows between 18 and 20 inches tall. Both the light green foliage and the stems are soft with down. This grass has been cultivated for centuries as it produces numerous terminal spikes of cottony fluff before the first killing frost kills the plants. It's always been a favorite for winter bouquets because the flower heads will not shatter with age. Sadly, their

very durability has led to unending mistreatment by people who dye the seedheads chartreuse or magenta, pop them in plastic vases, and sell them at highway rest stops.

(7) Champagne grass *(Rhynchelytrum repens)* will form large clumps of leaves up to four feet tall. Still called *Rhynchelytrum roseum* or *Tricholaena rosea* in seed catalogs that should know better, its other common names are ruby grass or natal grass. An annual in the North, it becomes a worrisome perennial whenever yearly temperatures stay above freezing. Floridians beware: this plant can become a pesky weed. The reddish-pink plumes turn a soft silver with age and are great cut flowers. They can be dried for winter bouquets, but use great care—they shatter easily. When gathering champagne grass, pull the stems rather than breaking or cutting them.

(8) Canary grass *(Phalaris canariensis)* grows three feet tall. A native of the Canary Islands and southern Europe, the plant is used to produce birdseed for both wild and domesticated canaries. Because the paper that lines the bottom of a birdcage often winds up at the local landfill, Canary grass is usually found at every such spot. The flower heads are a variegated green and yellowish white at the top of long and slender stems, but the plant itself is not at all attractive and should be kept to the cutting garden.

(9) Feathertop grass *(Pennisetum villosum)* is a two-to-three-foot-high annual in the North but perennial in the South. Often listed as *Pennisetum longistylum* in catalogs, the grass is floppy in appearance as the magnificent blossoms can be quite heavy. If picked before they open entirely, they can be dried for bouquets but they shatter easily with the slightest bump. Feathertop is most attractive as a cut flower and a lovely addition to any summer bouquet.

(10) Bearded wheat *(Triticum turgidum)* grows to four feet. The tradition of cultivating this hardy annual reaches far back in time. Its seeds are ground to become durum flour. Grown in most arid regions of the world because of its resistance to drought, the long seeds that appear to be bearded are unlike any others in the grass kingdom. The flowering stalks are a decorator's delight.

(11) Black sorghum *(Sorghum bicolor* var. *technicus)* will reach six feet in a good summer season. The sorghums have been used since prehistoric times and man has approached the species with an inventive mind. The sweet sap of some varieties is used for molasses, a second variety is used for making flour, a third is grown strictly for silage and cattle fodder, and a fourth is grown specifically for broomstraws. The shiny black seed heads of the specimen in the vase can spruce up floral arrangements. Even the cornlike leaves with their light green color deftly spattered with brown can be very effective when added to cut flowers. This is a very tender plant and should never be planted out before frost dangers are past.

(12) Foxtail grass *(Setaria lutescens)* will grow about two feet tall. It is a relative of foxtail millet and originally introduced as a common weed from Europe. It has become a common weed here, too. But the yellow-orange bristles of the seed heads are quite beautiful and retain their color after drying. In fact, a massive arrangement of 50 to 60 stems can cause even the most sophisticated gardener to ask where they are found and how much they cost.

(13) Job's tears *(Coix lacryma-jobi)* is a close relative of corn and will often grow to four feet in height. This plant has the distinction of being the oldest ornamental grass in cultivation—hardly a cloistered garden in the 14th century was without a row of these plants. The seeds fall readily from the plant at maturity and are very, very hard, colored with streaks of gray or black on white. The seeds are often utilized in the manufacture of rosaries. Job's tears will tolerate some shade and prefers a dampish spot in the garden. In colder climates start the seeds indoors to get a head start.

(14) Dragon's claw millet *(Eleusine coracana)* is an annual growing between two

Chasmanthium latifolium, *quaking oats, is planted here with nicotiana. Pick the panicles before they open for use in dried arrangements.*

and three feet tall. The heads resemble what could be a dragon's foot or the talons of a hefty bird. They also resemble something embroidered by a Victorian lady for a beaded purse. The grass is grown in Africa and Asia where it's called finger millet and used for flour and occasionally turned into a beer called *M'Poko.* Very good for dried bouquets, and unusual rather than beautiful in the garden.

(15) Wild oats *(Avena fatua)* grows up to four feet tall and is considered by most eastern farmers to be nothing but a troublesome weed. It can be found growing along many roadsides in high summer. Even for a grass the plants look straggly, but the flowers dry to a beautiful shade of light brown. A more civilized species called animated oats *(A. sterilis)* has a larger flower. The name animated refers to the needlelike spike that protrudes from the seed head and moves about as humidity changes.

If you would like to gather some grasses for winter bouquets, pick the stems on a dry and sunny day after the dews of morning have evaporated. Choose flowers that have not yet completely opened and cut the stems as long as you can—they can be trimmed later. Strip any excess leaves, tie small bunches of stems together, and hang them upside down on wire coat hangers, leaving plenty of air space between each bunch, in a cool, dry and airy room. Check the bundles every few days as the stems will shrink as they dry and some could fall to the floor and shatter. It should take between two and three weeks for the drying process.

Grasses from Seed to Plant

A nurseryman from North Carolina tells how to start many grasses from seed.

—P.L.

Majella Larochelle

Seeds of grasses must be collected at the proper time to ensure germination—usually when they begin to fall off the plant. Many species have a long hair (awn) at the end of the seed. When the awn appears, it is time to harvest the seed.

Discard any debris mixed with the seed, since often the decomposition of this vegetable matter leads to the rotting of the seed before it germinates. Store seed in a cool, dry place away from excessive heat and moisture.

Given the correct treatment at sowing, most grasses will germinate. Once sown, provide enough moisture to the seed pan. Continue to be careful about water after transplanting, since even grasses from the drylands of the world require ample moisture in the juvenile stage.

The following list gives various treatments of seed at the time of sowing.

Majella Larochelle is an expert in the study of seeds. He owns and operates a nursery headquartered in Asheville, North Carolina, and maintains a large seed collection, with specimens gathered from around the world. His selection of grass seeds is extensive.

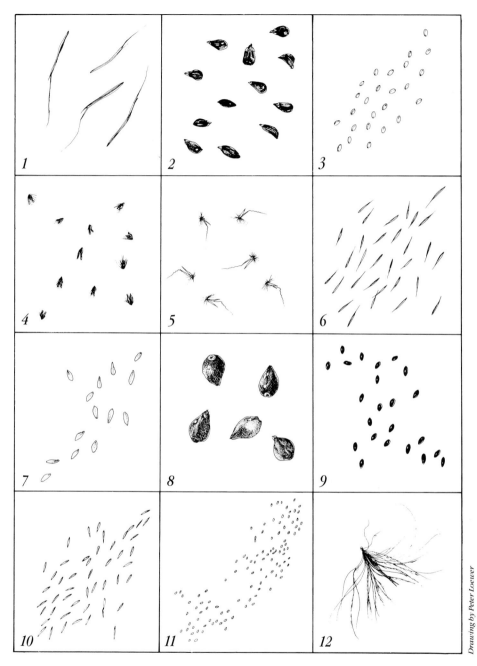

The accompanying illustration shows the seeds of 12 grasses at about actual size: (1) Bromus madritensis, (2) strawberry corn, (3) Setaria glauca, (4) champagne grass, (5) zebra grass, (6) Festuca glauca, (7) canary grass, (8) Job's tears. (9) black sorghum, (10) Koeleria glauca, (11) Eragrostis tef, (12) Pennisetum longistylum.

Easy to Germinate	Remarks	Easy to Germinate	Remarks
Aegilops ovata– annual goat grass	Germinates in 4 weeks.	*Bromus grandis*– brome grass	
Agropyron spicatum– bluebunch wheat grass	Germination variable.	*Bromus japonicus*– Japanese brome	
Agropyron trachycaulum– slender wheat grass		*Bromus vulgaris* var. *eximius*–brome grass	
Agrostis gigantea (A. alba)– red top		*Bromus lanceolatus (B. macrostachys)*– European brome	Germinates in 4 weeks.
Agrostis nebulosa– cloud grass	Germinates in 3 weeks outdoors.	*Bromus madritensis*– compact brome	Germinates in 4 weeks.
Agrostis stolonifera– bent grass	Give additional light.	*Bromus hordeaceus (B. mollis)* soft chess	
Aira caryophyllea–hairgrass			
Alopecurus pratensis– meadow foxtail	Give additional light during germination.	*Bromus* spp.– Brome grass	Give additional light during germination.
Ammophila breviligulata– American beach grass	Slow germination.	*Bromus tectorum* –downy brome	
Andropogon virginicus– broomsedge		*Buchloë dactyloides* –buffalo grass	Let the seed age before sowing.
Anthoxanthum odoratum– sweet vernal grass	Give additional light during germination.	*Calamovilfa longifolia*– prairie sandreed	
Aristida basiramea–forktip three-awn grass		*Carex buchananii*— leatherleaf sedge	Germinates in 4 weeks.
Aristida purpurea var- *longiseta*–Fendler three-awn grass	10-60 % germination.	*Carex muskingumensis*	
		Carex pseudo-cyperus	
Aristida purpurea– purple three-awn grass	10-60 % germination.	*Carex sylvatica*	
Arrhenatherum elatius– tall oat grass		*Coix lacryma-jobi*– Job's-tears	
Avena spp.–oats	Germinates in 3 weeks.	*Cortaderia selloana*– pampas grass	Germinates in 3 to 4 weeks at 70 °F.
Bouteloua curtipendula– side oats grama	Good germination if you keep the seed dry for 2 months.	*Corynophorus canescens*– gray hair grass	Slow germination.
Bouteloua eriopoda– black grama		*Cynosurus echinatus*– dog's-tail grass	Germinates in 4 weeks.
Bouteloua gracilis– blue grama		*Cyperus* spp.	Germinates in 4 weeks.
Bouteloua hirsuta– hairy grama		*Danthonia parryi*– parry oat grass	50 % germination.
Brachypodium sylvaticum– false brome	Slow germination.	*Deschampsia caespitosa*– tufted hair grass	Slow germination.
Briza maxima– big quaking grass	Germinates in 4 weeks.	*Echinochloa crus- galli*– barnyard grass	
Briza media– quaking grass	Slow germination.	*Eleocharis compressa* –spikerush	
Briza minor– little quaking grass		*Eleusine indica*– goose grass	Treat the seed first with 0.2 % potassium nitrate.
Bromus briziformis– rattlesnake chess	Germinates in 4 weeks.	*Elymus cinereus*– basin wildrye	Use full seed only.
Bromus unioloides– rescue grass		*Elymus glaucus*– blue wildrye	
		Elymus triticoides– beardless wildrye	

Easy to Germinate	Remarks	Easy to Germinate	Remarks
Eragrostis curvula-weeping love grass	Give additional light.	*Milium effusum*-wood millet	Germinates in 4 weeks.
Eragrostis spectabilis-purple love grass		*Miscanthus sacchariflorus*-Amur silver grass	
Eragrostis tef (E. abyssinica)-Teff	Germinates in 4 weeks.	*Miscanthus sinensis*-eulalia	
Eragrostis trichodes-Sand love grass		*Miscanthus sinensis* "New Hybrid"	True from seed.
Erianthus contortus-bent-awn plume grass	Slow germination.	*Muhlenbergia arenicola*-sand muhly	Poor germination.
Erianthus ravennae-ravenna grass		*Muhlenbergia cuspidata*-plains muhly	
Festuca amethystina-large blue fescue	Slow germination.	*Muhlenbergia glomerata*-green muhly	
Festuca gigantea-giant fescue	Slow germination.	*Muhlenbergia porteri*-bush muhly	Poor germination
Festuca cinerea	Slow generation.	*Muhlenbergia racemosa*-green muhly	
Festuca pulchella	Slow germination.	*Panicum capillare*-witch grass	Germinates in 4 weeks.
Glyceria striata-fowl manna grass		*Panicum clandestinum*-deertongue grass	
Hilaria belangeri-curly-mesquite	Use only fresh seed.	*Panicum dichotomiflorum*-fall panicum	Alternate daily warm & cold.
Hilaria jamesii-galleta grass	Use only fresh seed.	*Panicum lanuginosum*-hairy panic grass	
Hilaria mutica-tobosa grass	10-50 % germination.	*Panicum leibergii*-prairie panic grass	
Holcus lanatus-velvet grass	Give additional light during germination.	*Panicum linearifolium*-slimleaf panic grass	
Hordeum jubatum-squirreltail barley	Germinates in 2 weeks at 60 °F.	*Panicum miliaceum*-proso millet	Germinates in 4 weeks.
Hystrix patula-bottlebrush grass	Slow germination.	*Panicum obtusum*	Alternate daily warm & cold.
Juncus acutus-sharp rush		*Panicum virgatum*-switch grass	
Juncus alpinoarticulatus (J. alpinus)-alpine rush	Germinates in 2 weeks	*Paspalum dilatatum*-dallis grass	Treating the seed with potassium nitrate will help.
Koeleria glauca-large blue hair grass		*Paspalum urvillei*-vasey grass	Scarify the seed coat or treat the seed with potassium nitrate.
Lagurus ovatus-hare's-tail grass	Germinates in 3 weeks at 65 °F with fresh seed.	*Pennisetum flaccidum*	Slow germination.
Lamarckia aurea-goldentop	Germinates in 3 weeks.	*Pennisetum setaceum*-fountain grass	Germinates in 3 weeks at 70 °F.
Lolium multiflorum-Italian ryegrass		*Pennisetum villosum*-feathertop	Germinates in 3 weeks at 70 °F.
Luzula nivea-showy woodrush	Slow germination.	*Phalaris arundinacea*-reed canary grass	
Luzula pilosa-hairy woodrush	Slow germination.	*Phalaris canariensis*-canary grass	Germinates in 3 weeks.
Luzula sylvatica-great woodrush	Slow germination. True from seed.	*Phragmites australis (P. communis)*-common reed	Keep the seed wet.
Mibora minima-early sand grass	Germinates in 3 weeks at 50 °F.		
Milica ciliata-hairy melic grass	Slow germination.		

Easy to Germinate	Remarks
Poa alpina–alpine blue grass	
Poa chaxii–broad-leaved meadow grass	Slow germination.
Poa palustris–fowl meadow grass	
Poa sandbergii–Sandberg's blue grass	
Poa spp.–blue grass	Treat the seed with potassium nitrate.
Polypogon monspeliensis–rabbitfoot grass	Germinates in 4 weeks.
Rhynchelytrum repens—natal grass	Germinates in 4 weeks at 70° F.
Schizachyrium scoparium–little bluestem (*Andropogon scoparius*)	Slow germination.
Scirpus clintonii–bulrush	
Scirpus lacustris	Keep the seed wet.
Scirpus mucronatus	Slow germination.
Scirpus sylvaticus	Slow germination.
Sesleria autumnalis	Slow germination.
Sesleria heufleriana	
Setaria italica–foxtail millet	Germinates in 4 weeks.
Sitanion hystrix–squirreltail	
Sitanion jubatum–big squirreltail	
Sorghastrum nutans–Indian grass	Slow germination.
Sparganium minimum–bur-reed	Will take 2 months to germinate.
Spartina pectinata–prairie cord grass	
Sphenopholis obtusata var. *major (S. intermedia)*–wedge grass	
Spodiopogon sibiricus	Slow germination.
Sporobolus heterolepsis–prairie dropseed	
Stipa calamagrostis (Achnatherum calamagrostis)–silver grass	Slow germination.
Stipa capillata–feather grass	Slow germination.
Stipa coronata–crested stipa	
Stipa extremiorientialis–(*Achnatherum pekinense*)	Slow germination.
Stipa lettermani–Letterman needlegrass	
Stipa pulchra–purple needlegrass	

Easy to Germinate	Remarks
Stipa speciosa–desert needle grass	
Stipa tenacissima	Slow germination.
Stipa thurberiana–Thurber needle grass	Give additional light during germination.
Taeniatherum caput-medusae–medusa head	Keep in a warm place for first two weeks.
Themeda japonica	Slow germination.
Tridens flavus–tall redtop	
Triticum spp.–wheat	Germinates in 10-20 days.
Vulpia microstachys–small-fescue	
Vulpia octoflora–six-weeks-fescue	
Xerophyllum tenax–beargrass	Slow germination.
Zea mays–corn	Germinates in 2-4 weeks at 65° F.
Zizania aquatica–wild-rice	Germinates in 4 weeks.

Keep in a warm place for two to four weeks.	Remarks
Chasmanthium latifolium (Uniola latifolia)–spangle grass	
Eragrostis curvula var. *conferta*–Catalina Boer love grass	High germination.
Eragrostis lehmanniana–Lehmann love grass	High germination.
Luzula alopecurus	30 days to germinate.
Luzula lutea	30 days to germinate.
Pennisetum alopecuroides–fountain grass	
Sparganium erectum–branched bur-reed	
Typha angustifolia–narrow-leaved cat-tail	
Typha latifolia–common cat-tail	

Sow and keep in a cool place for at least one week.	Remarks
Aegilops kotschyi–goat grass	
Aegilops longissima–goat grass	Prefers calcareous soil.
Agrostis capillaris (A. tenuis)–colonial bent grass	Give additional light.
Andropogon gerardii–big bluestem	
Calamagrostis canadensis–bluejoint	Give additional light.
Carex spp.–Sedge	Give additional light.
Cenchrus ciliaris–buffel grass	Germination variable. Give additional light.
Dactylis glomerata–orchard grass	Give additional light.
Elymus canadensis–Canadian wildrye	
Festuca idahoensis–Idaho fescue	Poor germination. Give additional light.
Festuca ovina–sheep's fescue	May germinate in 2 weeks at 70 °F. Give additional light.
Hierochloë odorata–vanilla grass, sweet grass, holy grass	
Koeleria pyramidata–June grass	
Lolium spp.–ryegrass	Give additional light.
Melica stricta–rock melic grass	
Phleum pratense–Timothy	Give additional light.
Poa bulbosa–bulbous meadow grass	Treat the seed with potassium nitrate.
Puccinellia lemmonii–Lemmon's alkali grass	Poor germination. Treat the seed with potassium nitrate.
Sporobolus airoides–alkali sacaton	50 % germination. Give additional light.
Sporobolus asper–rough dropseed	
Sporobolus cryptandrus–sand dropseed	Give additional light.
Sporobolus giganteus–giant dropseed	50 % germination. Give additional light.
Stipa spartea–porcupine grass	
Trisetum spicatum–spike trisetum	Variable. Give additional light.

Give six weeks of cold followed by one month of warm.	Remarks
Andropogon hallii–sand bluestem	Give additional light.
Carex acuta (C. gracilis)–slender tufted sedge	
Carex grayi	
Carex pendula (C. maxima)–pendulous sedge	
Carex punctata–dotted sedge	
Helictotrichon sempervirens (Avena s.)–blue oat grass	
Juncus ensifolius	
Molinia caerulea subsp. *arundinacea*	
Molinia caerulea–purple moor grass	
Psathyrostachys junceus (Elymus junceus)	Give additional light.
Stipa barbata	
Stipa pennata–European feather grass	
Stipa viridula–green needle grass	Poor germination. Give additional light.

Seed scarification or acid treatment will help	Remarks
Danthonia spicata–poverty oat grass	50 % germination
Oryzopsis hymenoides–Indian ricegrass	
Stipa comata–needle-and-thread grass	

Give additional light during germination	Remarks
Agropyron smithii–Western wheat grass	Poor germination without a potassium nitrate soaking.
Agrostis canina–velvet bent grass	Treat the seed with potassium nitrate.
Agrostis gigantea–redtop	Treat the seed with potassium nitrate
Chloris gayana (A. alba)–rhodes grass	Treat the seed with potassium nitrate.
Cynodon dactylon–Bermuda grass	Irregular. Treat the seed with potassium nitrate.

Annual Grasses

Botanical Name	Common Name	Height	Flowering Period	Sources*
Agrostis nebulosa	Cloud grass	18″	4–10 wks.	2, 7
Avena sterilis	Animated oats	3′	4–6 wks.	5, 7
Briza maxima	Quaking grass	2′	6–10 wks.	2, 6, 7
Briza minor	Little quaking grass	9–12″	4–6 wks.	2, 4, 7
Bromus lanceolatus (B. macrostachys)	Brome grass	2′	6–10 wks.	2
Coix lacryma-jobi	Job's-tears	2–3′	10+ wks.	4, 6, 7
Eragrostis elegans	Love grass	18–24″	10+ wks.	4, 7
Hordeum jubatum	Squirreltail-barley	18–24″	6 wks.	2, 7
Lagurus ovatus	Hare's-tail grass	12–18″	10+ wks.	2, 4, 6, 7
Lamarckia aurea	Goldentop	1′	6–10 wks.	4
Leptochloa fascicularis	Spike grass	2½′	6–10 wks.	4
Panicum miliaceum (P. violaceum)	Panic grass	3′	6–10 wks.	7
Pennisetum setaceum (P. ruppelii)	Fountain grass	4′	10+ wks.	1, 6
Pennisetum villosum (P. longistylum)	Feathertop	2′	6–10 wks.	7
Phalaris canariensis	Canary grass	2–4′	4–6 wks.	2, 7
Polypogon monspeliensis	Rabbitfoot grass	18″	6–10 wks.	7
Rhynchelytrum repens (syn. Tricholaena roseum)	Natal grass	1–2′	10+ wks.	4, 7
Setaria lutescens (S. glauca)	Glaucous bristle grass, yellow bristle grass	18–30″	10+ wks.	7
Setaria italica	Foxtail millet	2′	6–10 wks.	4
Triticum spelta	Spelt wheat	2′	4–6 wks.	2, 7
Triticum turgidum (T. durum)	Durum wheat	2′	4–6 wks.	2

Selected Sources for Ornamental Grasses

1) Kurt Bluemel, Inc., Nurseries, 2543 Hess Rd., Fallston, MD 21047;

2) The Country Garden, Rt. 2, Crivitz, WI 54114;

3) Endangered Species, Box 1830, Tustin, CA 92681-1830;

4) J.L. Hudson, Box 1058, Redwood City, CA 94064;

5) Logee's Greenhouses, 55 North St., Danielson, CT 06239;

6) Park Seed Co., Greenwood, SC 29647-0001;

7) Thompson and Morgan, Box 1308, Jackson NJ 08527;

8) Wayside Gardens, Hodges, SC 29695-0001.

References

Grounds, Roger. *Ornamental Grasses.* New York: Van Nostrand Reinhold, 1981.

Loewer, H. Peter. *Growing and Decorating with Grasses.* New York: Walker and Company, 1977.

Meyer, Mary Hockenberry. *Ornamental Grasses.* New York: Charles Scribner's Sons, 1975.

Chart Codes

Form		Uses			
I	= Irregular	S	= Sun	E	Edging
M	= Mound	PSh	= Partial shade	DS	= Dry soil
OS	= Open-spreading	Sh	= Shade	MS	= Moist soil
T	= Tufted	Sp	= Specimen	RG	= Rock garden
UA	= Upright-arching	G	= Groups	FC	= Fall color
UN	= Upright-narrow	M	= Massing	DF	= Decorative flowers
UO	= Upright-open	Sc	= Screen	N	= Naturalizing
		GC	= Ground cover		

Perennial Grasses

USDA

Hardiness Zone	Botanical Name	Common Name	Ht.	Form*	Uses*	Sources*
6–7	*Alopecurus lanatus*	Wooly foxtail	1'	T	S, RG	1
6–9	*Alopecurus pratensis* 'Aureus'	Yellow foxtail, meadow foxtail	1'	T-UO	S, G, M, RG	1
4–9	*Andropogon gerardii* (See Schizachyrium/ scoparium)	Big blue stem	4–6'	UA	S, G, M	
4–9	*Anthoxanthum odoratum*	Sweet vernal grass	2'	UA–UN	S, DS	4
4–9	*Arrhenatherum elatius bulbosum* 'Variegatum'	Bulbous oat grass	1–2'	T-UO	S, PSh, M, RG	1
7–10	*Arundo donax*	Giant reed	9–12'	UA–UO	S, Sp, Sc, DF	1
8–10	*Arundo donax* 'Variegata'	Striped giant reed	5–7'	UA–UO	S, Sp, Sc	1
4–9	*Bouteloua curtipendula*	Side oats grama	2–3'	UA–UN	S, M	1
4–9	*Bouteloua gracilis*	Blue grama	1–2'	T-UO	S, G, RG, N, DF	1
4–8	*Briza media*	Quaking grass	2–3'	UO	S, M, N, DF	1,2
6–9	*Bromus ramosus*	Brome grass	3–4'	T	S, PSh, G	1
5–9	*Calamagrostis acutiflora stricta*	Feather reed grass	5–7'	UA–UN	S, G	1, 8
6–9	*Calamagrostis* x *arundinacea brachytricha*	Korean reed grass	2–3'	UA–UN	S,PSh, G	1
6–8	*Chascolytrum subaristatum* (Syn. Briza subaristata)	Quaking grass	1'	UA–UN	S, RG	1
5–9	*Chasmanthium latifolium* (Syn. Uniola)	Spangle grass	3–5'	UA–UN	Sh, G, M, N, FC	1
8–10	*Cortaderia richardii* (Syn C. conspicua)	Black pampas	5–10'	UN–UO	S, Sp, Sc, DF	1
8–10	*Cortaderia selloana*	Pampas grass	8–12'	UN–UO	S, Sp, Sc, DF	1, 4, 6, 8
8–10	*Cortaderia selloana* 'Argenteum'	Silvery blooming pampas grass	9–12'	UN–UO	S, Sp, DF, Sc	1
7–10	*Cortaderia selloana* 'Rendatleri'	Pink pampas grass	8–10'	UN–UO	S, Sp, DF, Sc	8
8–10	*Cortaderia selloana* 'Rosa Feder'	Pink pampas grass	9–12'	UN–UO	S, Sp,DF, Sc	1
8–10	*Cortaderia selloana* 'Sunningdale Silver'	Pampas grass	6–9'	UN–UO	S, Sp, Sc, DF	1
8–10	*Cortaderia selloana* 'Pumila'	Compact pampas grass	4–6'	UN–UO	S, Sp, DF	1
9–10	*Cymbopogon citratus*	Lemon grass	3–6'	I–UA	S, Sp, G	1
5–9	*Dactylis glomerata* 'Variegata'	Cock's-foot orchard grass	1–2'	UO	S, PSh, G, E	1
4–9	*Deschampsia caespitosa*	Tufted hair grass	2'	T-M	S, PSh, G, M, RG, N, DF	1
4–9	*Deschampsia caespitosa* 'Bronzeschleier'		3'	T-M	S, PSh, G, M	1
4–9	*Deschampsia caespitosa* 'Goldgehaenge'		3'	T-M	S, PSh, G, M	1
6–9	*Deschampsia caespitosa* 'Goldschleier'		2–3'	T-M	S, PSh, G, M	1
6–9	*Deschampsia caespitosa* 'Goldstaub'		2–3'	T-M	S, PSh, G, M	1
4–9	*Deschampsia caespitosa* 'Schottland'	Scottish tufted hair grass	4–6'	T-M	S, PSh, G, M	1
4–9	*Deschampsia caespitosa* 'Tautraeger'		3'	T-M	S, PSh, G, M	1
4–9	*Deschampsia caespitosa tardiflora*	Late-blooming tufted hair grass	3'	T-M	S, PSh, G, M	1
4–9	*Deschampsia flexuosa*	Crinkled hair grass	2½'	T-UO	S, PSh, RG, DF	4

Perennial Grasses

USDA Hardiness Zone	Botanical Name	Common Name	Ht.	Form*	Uses*	Sources*
5–9	*Deschampsia caespitosa vivipara* 'Fairy's Joke'	Viviparous hair grass	3'	T	S, PSh, G, M	1
5–9	*Elymus* 'Vahl Glaucus' (Syn. Leymus racemosus)	Giant blue wildrye	3–6'	UA	S, G, M	1
4–9	*Elymus glaucus*	Blue wildrye	2–4'	I	S, G, GC	1
7–9	*Erianthus contortus*	Bent-awn plume grass	5–6'	UC	S, PSh, MS	1
7–9	*Erianthus giganteus*	Sugarcane plume grass	3–9'	UO	S, Sp, G	1
6–9	*Erianthus ravennae*	Ravenna grass	9–12'	UO	S, Sp, Sc, DF	1
7–9	*Erianthus strictus*	Narrow plume grass	3–6'	T-UN	S, G, M	1
4–8	*Festuca amethystina* 'April Gruen'	Olive-green fescue	8"	T	S, M, GC, RG	1, 3
4–8	*Festuca amethystina* 'Bronzeglanz'	Bronze fescue	8"	T	S, M, GC, RG	1, 3
4–9	*Festuca cinerea superba*	Blue fescue	6"	T	S, M, E	1
4–9	*Festuca ovina glauca*	Dwarf blue fescue	8–12"	T	S, M, E, RG, GC	4, 6, 7
5–8	*Glyceria maxima* 'Variegata'	Manna grass	2–3'	I	S, M	1
7–9	*Hakonechloa macra* (Syn. Phragmites macra)		2'	M	PSh, G, GC	
7–9	*Hakonechloa macra* 'Aureola'	Golden variegated hakonechloa	1–2'	M	PSh, G, M, GC	1, 3
4–8	*Helictotrichon sempervirens* (Syn. Avena)	Blue oat grass	2'	T	S, G, M, RG	1
5–9	*Holcus lanatus*	Velvet grass	1–3'	UA–UN	S, G	1

See p. 96 for keys to form, use and source codes.

The Conservatory Garden in New York contains a mixture of grasses and perennials to produce a striking border.

Perennial Grasses

USDA Hardiness Zone	Botanical Name	Common Name	Ht.	Form*	Uses*	Sources*
7–9	*Holcus lanatus* 'Variegatus'	Variegated velvet grass	8″	T–OS	S, PSh, G, GC, RG	1
5–6	*Hystrix patula*	Bottlebrush grass	3′	UO	S, PSh, G, M, N, DF	1
7–9	*Imperata cylindrica rubra*	Japanese bloodgrass	1–2′	M–OS	S, PSh, G, M	1, 3
6–8	*Koeleria lobata* (Syn. K. brevis)	Blue hair grass	4″	T–UN	S, N, RG	1
6–9	*Koeleria glauca*	Large blue hair grass	1′	T–UO	S, G, M, RG	1, 4, 7
5–9	*Melica ciliata*	Hairy melic grass	1–2′	T	S, PSh, G	1, 7
4–9	*Melica transsilvanica*	Transylvanian melic grass	1–2′	T	S, PSh, G	4, 7
7–9	*Milium effusum*	Wood millet	2′	T	PSh, G, DF	1
7–9	*Milium effusum aureum*	Golden wood millet	2′	UO	PSh, G, DF	1, 7
6–9	*Miscanthus sinensis*	Eulalia	6–8′	UO	S, PSh, G, M, N, S, DF	1
6–9	*Miscanthus sinensis* 'Gracillimus'		5–8′	UA	S, Sp, G, DF	1, 8
7–9	*Miscanthus sinensis purpurascens*		3–4′	UN–UO	S, Sp, G, DF	1, 8
6–9	*Miscanthus sinensis* 'Variegatus'	Variegated eulalia	5–7′	UO	S, PSh, S, G, MS, DF	1
6–9	*Miscanthus sinensis* 'Zebrinus'	Zebra eulalia	6–8′	UN–UO	S, Sp, G, MS, DF	1, 3, 8
4–9	*Molinia caerulea* 'Variegata'	Variegated purple moor grass	2′	T–UA	S, PSh, G, M, GC, RG	1, 3, 8
9–10	*Oplismenus hirtellus* 'Variegatus'	Ribbon grass	2–3′	OS	S, GC	5
5–9	*Panicum clandestinum*	Deertongue grass	3–4′	UN	PSh, MS	1
5–9	*Panicum virgatum*	Switch grass	5–8′	UN	S, G, M, Sc FC, DF, N	1
5–9	*Panicum virgatum* 'Rotstrahlbusch'	Red switch grass	3–4′	UN	S, MS, G	1
5–9	*Panicum virgatum strictum*	Tall switch grass	5–6′	UN–UA	S, MS, G	1
6–9	*Pennisetum alopecuroides*	Fountain grass	3–4′	M	S, G, M, DF	1
7–9	*Pennisetum orientale*	Orient fountain grass	2–3′	T	S, G, M	1
4–9	*Phalaris arundinacea picta* (Syn. P.a. variegata)	Ribbon grass, gardener's-garters	2–3′	UO	S, PSh, M, G	1
4–8	*Schizachyrium scoparium* (Syn. Andropogon scoparius)	Little blue stem	3′	UA–UN	S, G, M	1
6–9	*Sorghastrum nutans* (Syn. S. avenaeum)	Indian grass	4–6′	UO	S, G, M, N FC, DF	1, 2, 4
5–9	*Spartina pectinata*	Prairie cord grass	4–6′	UA–UO	S, MS, E, G, M, N	1
5–9	*Spartina pectinata* 'Aurea Variegata'	Variegated cord grass	5–7′	UA–UO	S, MS, FC, G, M, DF	1, 3
7–10	*Stenotaphrum secundatum* 'Variegatum'	Striped St. Augustine grass	3–12″	OS	S, GC, RG	5
6–9	*Stipa capillata*	Feather grass	3–4′	UO	S, DS, G, DF	1, 6
7–9	*Stipa gigantea*	Giant feather grass	4–6′	T	S, Sp, G	1, 8
7–9	*Stipa pennata*	European feather grass	4–5′	UO	S, DS, G, DF	1, 4, 7
7–9	*Themeda triandra* 'Japonica'	Japanese themeda	4–5′	UN	S, Sp, G, FC	1

A Problem with Pampas Grass

Recently a letter to an English gardening magazine asked: When is the best time to dig up and move a large pampas grass and how do you do it?

The surprising answer was: The best time is during the winter. Before digging up the plant, remove as much of the old foliage as possible. The traditional method is to light a small bonfire in it to burn it off. Screwing up several sheets of newspaper beneath the plant should provide sufficient heat and flame to burn off all the top growth. Then simply lift the roots with as much soil as possible and replant. It can also be divided if you wish.

Sources for Ornamental Grasses

The list (pp 96-99) covers the majority—but not all—of the ornamental grasses available to today's gardener. For additional sources of seeds of the more unusual grasses (including rushes, sedges, and grass look-a-likes) gardeners are advised to join the various rock garden societies including:

The American Rock Garden Society
15 Fairmead Rd., Darien, CT 06820

The Scottish Rock Garden Club
21 Merchiston Park, Edinburgh, EH10 4PW, Scotland, U.K.

The Alpine Garden Society
Lye End Link, St. John's, Woking, Surrey, England

The Royal Horticultural Society
Vincent Square, London SW1P 2PE U.K.

And the following additional firms for seeds:
Chiltern Seeds, Bortree Stile, Ulverston, Cumbria U.K. LA12 7PB.
Stock Seed Farms, Inc., R.R. #1, Box 112, Mursock, Nebraska 68407.
Thompson & Morgan, P.O. Box 1380, Jackson, New Jersey 08527.

and additional sources of plants:

Garden Place, 6780 Heisley Road, P.O. Box 83, Mentor, OH 44060.
Prairie Nursery, P.O. Box 365, Westerfield, WI 53964
Tripple Brook Farm, 37 Middle Road, Southampton, MA 01073
Sandy Mush Herbs, Rte. 2, Surrett Cove Road, Leicester, NC 28748.

Pennisetum setaceum *'Rubrum' is a dramatic accent for any garden providing color and grace.*

Drawing by Peter Loewer

Bamboos at Brooklyn Botanic Garden

October 1988

Scientific Name	Common Name	C = Clumping R = Running Habit	Location
Arundinaria variegata		R	Bonsai Nursery
Arundinaria viridistriata		R	Bonsai Nursery
Bambusa 'Chinese Golden Bamboo'		C	Greenhouse
Bambusa glaucescens var. *riviereorum*	Chinese-goddess bamboo	C	Aquatic Greenhouse
Bambusa tuldoides	Punting-pole bamboo	C	Tropical Greenhouse
Bambusa vulgaris	Common bamboo	C	Greenhouse
Bambusa vulgaris 'Vittata'	Jade-striped golden bamboo	C	Conservatory Entry
Phyllostachys sp.*	Phyllostachys (bamboo)	R	Witch-hazel Island
*Phyllostachys arcana**	Phyllostachys (bamboo)	R	Japanese Garden
Phyllostachys aurea	Golden bamboo	R	Greenhouse
*Phyllostachys aureosulcata**	Yellow-groove bamboo	R	Japanese Garden
*Phyllostachys bissetii**	David Bisset bamboo	R	West Conifer Collection
*Phyllostachys flexuosa**	Zigzag bamboo	R	Japanese Garden
Phyllostachys nidularia 'Smooth-sheath'*	Broom bamboo	R	Japanese Garden
*Phyllostachys nigra**	Black bamboo	R	Greenhouse; SE Oak Circle
*Phyllostachys nuda**	Phyllostachys (bamboo)	R	Japanese Garden
*Phyllostachys rubromarginata**	Phyllostachys (bamboo)	R	Japanese Garden
Pleioblastus chino var. *viridis* f. *humilis**	Azuma-Nezasa (bamboo)	R	SE Oak Circle
*Pleioblastus variegatus**	Dwarf whitestripe bamboo	R	Japanese Garden
*Pseudosasa japonica**	Arrow bamboo or Metake	R	West Willow Area
Pseudosasa japonica var. *tsutsumiana**	Arrow bamboo (cultivar)	R	SE Oak Circle
Sasa veitchii 'Nana'*	Yakibazasa (bamboo)	R	Japanese Garden
*Shibataea kumasasa**	Ruscus-leaved bamboo	R	Japanese Garden

*BBG is in Zone 7 (USDA Hardiness Zone Map), low temperature Zero degrees F.

Bamboos Recommended for Bonsai

Chimonobambusa marmorea (kanchiku)
Pleioblastus pygmaeus (oroshimachiku)
Pseudosasa japonica (yadake)
Sasa palmata nebulosa (shakotanchiku)
Sasa veitchii (kumazasa)

Larger Bamboos for Pots

Bambusa multiplex (horaichiku)
Phyllostachys aurea (hoteichiku)
Phyllostachys nigra (kurochiku)
Semiarundinaria fastuosa (narihiradake)

Top left, Carex grayi *and below,* C. pendula—*two graceful sedges. Grow in fertile soil in sun or part shade. Best grown as specimen plants.*

Grasslike plants

Kerry Barringer

In addition to the hundreds of grasses in cultivation, there are a few plants that look like grasses, but are not. Blue-eyed grass, *Sisyrinchium,* is in the iris family, onion grass, *Allium,* is a true onion, pin grass, *Erodium cicutaria,* is a relative of the geraniums, and starry grass, *Cerastium arvense,* is a relative of the carnations. There are many more. It is usually easy to tell these plants from the true grasses by their showy flowers, but plants in the sedge family, Cyperaceae, and the rush family, Juncaceae, also have inconspicuous flowers and can be difficult to tell from grasses. A few of the species in these families are in cultivation. Because of their preference for wet or water-logged soil, they are used along ponds and in damp wildflower gardens as well as in aquaria.

The sedges have stems that are triangular in cross-section and you can feel the angles if you roll the stems between your fingers. In contrast, the grasses have rounded stems. On some sedges, the angles are slightly rounded and can be difficult to distinguish. If this is the case, you must look at the lower part of the leaf, called the sheath, that clasps the stem. Sedges have sheaths that are closed tubes while grasses have sheaths that are slit along one side. You can gently pull a blade of grass so that the sheath comes away from the stem, but no amount of tugging will separate a sedges' sheath without tearing it.

Some of the sedges are popular water garden plants. The umbrella sedge, *Cyperus alternifolius,* is a native of Africa and Madagascar. It has a brushlike clusters of leaves and flowering branches borne at the top of slender stems. The papyrus, *Cyperus papyrus,* and its dwarf relative, *Cyperus isocladus,* can form dramatic clumps but must be watched because it can spread rapidly by underground stems.

Though seldom planted, the species of *Carex* can be attractive along the edges of ponds and in wildflower gardens. Species like the European *Carex pendula* and the native *Carex crinita* have lovely pendent spikes borne at the top of gently arching stems. The evergreen *Carex plantaginea* can be an interesting rock garden subject with its broad leaves and its purple-bracted flower stalks and the white-striped leaves of *Carex morrowii* var. *expallida,*the Japanese sedge, can add an unusual touch to borders.

The rushes, all in the genus *Juncus,* have small onionlike flowers but their petals and sepals have the color and texture of grass leaves. Very few are grown. They usually have wiry stems with a few thin leaves at the base and a few flowers near the top. Like the sedges, most species prefer wet, shady sites.

The Japanese-mat rush, *Juncus effusus,* is intensively cultivated in Japan where it is used to weave the tatami mats that are the usual floor covering in Japanese homes. *Juncus tenuis,* the path rush, is often an unwelcome guest in gardens but the species is remarkable for its toughness and tenacity. The path rush is often the only plant growing in paths and parking lots where the soil is constantly being trampled or compressed. It adds a little green to even the most desolate sites. The wood rush, *Luzula campestris,* is a broad-leaved relative of the rushes that is sometimes used in wildflower gardens. This clump-forming perennial has stems and leaves covered with long, white hairs. Plants reappear early in the spring and reach their full growth before leaves appear on the trees.

There are thousands of species of sedges and rushes growing wild in the world. They are usually overlooked as garden subjects, but they thrive in the damp shady areas that other species shun and can be useful in the poorly-drained corner of the garden where an interesting or unusual accent is sought.